Foiled

Personal Story Publishing Project Series

    Bearing Up, 2018
    - making do, bearing up, and overcoming adversity

    Exploring, 2019
    - discoveries, challenges, and adventures

    That Southern Thing, 2020
    - living, loving, laughing, loathing, leaving the South

    Luck and Opportunity, spring 2021
    - between if and if only

    Trouble, fall 2021
    - causing, avoiding, getting in, and getting out

    Curious Stuff, spring 2022
    - mementos, treasures, white elephants, and junk

    Twists and Turns, fall 2022
    - inflection points in life by choice, happenstance, misfortune, failure, and grace

    Lost & Found, spring 2023
    - loss and discovery—trials, serendipity, and life after

    Sooner or Later, fall 2023
    - about time, timing, and inevitability

    Now or Never, spring 2024
    - about courage and regret, danger and desire, about choosing

    Foolhardy, fall 2024
    - about derring-do, desperation, and disaster—or not

Available through Daniel Boone Footsteps
www.danielboonefootsteps.com
www.RandellJones.com
1959 N. Peace Haven Rd., #105
Winston-Salem, NC 27106

Foiled

Randell Jones, editor

Daniel Boone Footsteps
Winston-Salem, North Carolina

Copyrights retained by each writer for own stories
Permissions granted to Daniel Boone Footsteps
for publishing in this anthology

Compilation Copyright 2025, Daniel Boone Footsteps
All Rights Reserved
ISBN: 979-8-9902784-3-1

Daniel Boone Footsteps
1959 N. Peace Haven Rd., #105
Winston-Salem, NC 27106

RandellJones.com
DanielBooneFootsteps.com
DBooneFootsteps@gmail.com

Cover image courtesy of *Mrs. Knight's Smartest Artists*

"the best laid schemes o' mice and men gang aft agley,"

— Robert Burns from "To a Mouse"

Preface

This book is the 12th in a series of anthologies, collections of personal stories on a set theme, our Personal Story Publishing Project. Since beginning in 2018, our collections have included these titles:

Bearing Up,   *Twists and Turns,*
Exploring,   *Lost & Found,*
That Southern Thing, *Sooner or Later,*
Luck and Opportunity, *Now or Never, and*
Trouble,   *Foolhardy.*
Curious Stuff,

This book comes from our 12th Call for Personal Stories, this one on the theme: "Foiled—personal stories of great expectations gone awry by surprise, shortsightedness, and trickery."

We thank the scores of writers who responded to the call by submitting such interesting, thoughtful, and well-crafted stories. They delivered the diversity and depth of perspective we were hoping for and the insight to self which proved we chose the right theme. Each story is about 750-800 words, so the writers were challenged in executing their craft, telling an interesting story succinctly. The writers and we have all found the Personal Story Publishing Project through its 12 iterations, so far, to be an instructive and rewarding writing experience. For the readers, it is a delight.

We received submissions from many writers in North Carolina and across the South, notably, but also from writers reaching across the country from Florida, Pennsylvania, New York, New Jersey, Connecticut, Colorado to the West Coast. We wish we could have printed them all, but we are delighted to curate 44 stories for this collection.

In June 2019, we launched a second outlet for sharing these fine writers with a broader audience. Their work can now be heard in our twice weekly podcast, "6-minute Stories." Our podcast is available through Apple Podcasts (iTunes) and Spotify. You can listen directly to "6-minute Stories" and find all the stories archived at RandellJones.com/6minutestories. Episodes are announced on Facebook @6minutestories.

Foiled, the Personal Story Publishing Project, and "6-minute Stories" podcast are undertaken by author and publisher Randell Jones, doing business as Daniel Boone Footsteps in Winston-Salem, North Carolina.

Thank you for enjoying and appreciating good storytelling. And, remember…

Everybody loves a good story.sm •

— RJ

Contents

Preface	vii
Contents	ix-xiv
Introduction	xv

Auld Lang Syne   1
    by Jamie Cheshire, Winston-Salem, NC
    — *In the cold twilight above the town, he sang it to himself.*

Digging for Foo-Foo Dust   5
    by Vicki Easterly, Frankfort, KY
    — *DIG! DIG! FLY! FLY!*

The (sorta kinda) Runaway   9
    by Jo McElroy Senecal, Mount Pleasant, SC
    — *Who does this?*

Mom Won't Like It   13
    by Edward von Koenigseck, Ticonderoga, NY
    — *"Jane can't ever know the truth."*

First Love   17
    by David Lusk, Winston-Salem, NC
    — *I had a secret power—a newfound ally.*

Daddy's Girl   21
    by Willow Noelle Groskreutz, Mooresville, NC
    — *"Isn't your dad like a cult leader?"*

The Recliner   25
    by Anne Anthony, Chapel Hill, NC
    – *The stare-off begins. Puss-faces, Mom called us.*

Love Finds a Way   29
    by Barbara Reese Yager, Fort Mill, SC
    – *"How can you give him up? He seems devoted to you."*

Yeses   33
    by Richard L. Davis, Elk Grove, CA
    – *how about us living two years in central Africa?*

Vacation   37
    by Eloise Currie, Raleigh, NC
    – *The change is unnerving.*

Take the Girls Seriously   41
    by Mary Clements Fisher, Cupertino, CA
    – *"Oh, little sister, that's enough out of you."*

Behind Lace Curtains   45
    by Valerie Macon, Fuquay-Varina, NC
    – *Leaving the door ajar, she darted out in her bathrobe.*

A Landlubber's Tale   49
    by Arlene Mandell, Linville, NC
    – *We liked each other. We needed to find common ground.*

Shooting Stars   53
    by Anne M. Middleton, Raleigh, NC
    – *Drew and I became "a thing."*

Feline Education   57
    by Tanya E. E. E. Schmid, Semione, Switzerland
    — *"Pete!" I call out, knowing snakes are deaf.*

My Father Figure   61
    by Akira Odani, St. Augustine, FL
    — *With a friendly smile, he joked, "You caught a big fish!"*

Just a Doodle?   65
    by Janice Luckey, Mooresville, NC
    — *"If the test was positive, what would I do about it?"*

Just Desserts   69
    by Robin Russell Gaiser, Asheville, NC
    — *"I'll take care of this, Honey."*

Strike Up the Band   73
    by Joel R. Stegall, Winston-Salem, NC
    — *whatever enlisted men played, or claimed to play, an instrument*

The Truth Comes Out   77
    by Joel R. Stegall, Winston-Salem, NC
    — *I respected the officer and assumed he would also respect me.*

Stuck in the Second Stage   81
    by Kym B. Whitecar, Indian Trail, NC
    — *My warped resentment started after Dad died.*

The Perfect Imperfect   85
    by Alison Rice Bruster, Fort Mill, SC
    — *That was the plan, anyway.*

A Christmas Surprise   89
    by Annette L. Brown, Atwater, CA
    — *"Sweetheart, wake up! Santa's here!"*

Choices About Love   93
    by Ginny Foard, Sullivan's Island, SC
    — *"You've got to do something about this," they jibed him.*

Going for the Gold   97
    by Thomas Gery, Reading, PA
    — *"I can do that."*

Operation New TV   101
    by Lisa Williams Kline, Davidson, NC
    — *"Let's do it ourselves."*

We Thought We Were Safe Here   105
    by Beth Bixby Davis, Fletcher, NC
    — *I felt a giant hug, surrounded by these beautiful mountains.*

If We Could Just Get Married   109
    by Lorraine Martin Bennett, Hayesville, NC
    — *"I drove your car off a mountain."*

Unseen Troubles   113
    by Marcia J. Wick, Colorado Springs, CO
    — *Nothing would deter us from enjoying our evening out.*

Not a Suitable Suitor   117
    by Suzanne Cottrell, Oxford, NC
    — *"Can we keep one?"*

Four-minute Showers   121
    by Dawn McCormack, Plainfield, CT
    — *"I cleaned it up, Mommy."*

Fire and Rain   125
    by Kristen Bryson, Charlotte, NC
    — *"Do you have any questions?"*

With a Lump in My Throat   129
    by Marion Cohen, Cherry Hill, NJ
    — *I just kept working every day, knowing I would adjust.*

Tequila or Not Tequila   133
    by Jeanne VanBuren, Winston-Salem, NC
    — *What have you got in a red?*

Dream-catching   137
    by Jane Satchell McAllister, Mocksville, NC
    — *Buona fortuna.*

The Water Tower   141
    by Annie McLeod Jenkins, Winston-Salem, NC
    — *because it was there—our Mt. Everest.*

Chasing the Great Comet   145
    by S. G. Benson, Warne, NC
    — *"We can't let her know what we're up to."*

Ride-sharing, Old School   149
    by Barbara Mueller, Asheville, NC
    — *After that, my confidence in strangers diminished.*

Taste the Disappointment   153
       by Joe Brown, Bethania, NC
         – *There's almost no food that I don't like.*

Tenderfoot   157
       by Bob Amason, St. Augustine, FL
         – *"Let's go backpacking."*

We Got Five Done   161
       by Howard Pearre, Winston-Salem, NC
         – *"Okay, Mr. Spark Plug. Out you come."*

Close Call   165
       by Erika Hoffman, Chapel Hill, NC
         – *"This isn't a timeshare. Our program's based on points."*

Proper Punishment for an Old Offender   169
       by Paula Teem Levi, Clover, SC
         – *"The inmates here are an army of forgotten men."*

A Debt of Gratitude   173
       by Randell Jones, Winston-Salem, NC
         – *I just wanted to say, "thank you."*

Introduction

Foiled—something intended, something attempted, has not come about. It has not been accomplished as we might have envisioned, might have hoped. Those on either side of that turning point might feel differently about that faulty outcome. *We foiled a robbery. An outbreak of flu foiled our plans for the class reunion.* Such an interruption can be a good thing or a bad thing. It all depends.

And the causes of that interruption can vary as well. Were we caught off guard, completely surprised, subject to the whims of fate and chance? Or perhaps we embarked on a course of action without sufficient forethought. Did we begin on a lark, deciding what to do next on the fly, short on contingency plans? Or was something nefarious—or at least someone mischievous—involved? A prank, a trick, a scheme—a fraud, even—might have our plans crashing down around our heads or, at the least, just not living up to our expectations, be they reasonable or otherwise.

Ah, yes, our "expectations." That's how we get through life, isn't it? We learn from the beginning the way the world works—what we can do to get ourselves fed, cleaned up, and hugged. We learn who we are and how we fit into the world and how to navigate that "system." And then we begin to think "what if," wondering what we might do, could do. We toss some of those thoughts into the bin we've labeled "wants" and categorize some further into "desires" and "wouldn't-it-be-greats." Those are the ones that set us up for adventure, challenge, accomplishment, disappointment, and more. Our hopes and dreams and our "what-ifs" become our great expectations. And having those is, in fact, why we have stories.

We are delighted by the response to our 12th Call for Personal Stories, and we are thankful to all the writers who invested time and energy into crafting personal stories for possible inclusion in this anthology. From among the submissions, we chose stories to include based on the quality of the writing and the resonance of the personal experiences shared with the announced theme, "Foiled—personal stories of great expectations gone awry by surprise, short-sightedness, and trickery."

We have stories of surprise, of course—the Santa-siting so cleverly planned, the fury of wind and rain destroying paradise, a door that dared to latch behind the not-quite-dressed parent of a toddler, and the family's international year abroad interrupted by political revolution.

We have stories of dreamers—one jumping into a bad job because the money looked so good, another spawning a life-long ambition from an early disappointment. One story has a dog-lover counting his puppies before he learns the truth of animal husbandry. And a couple with their adventurous travel plans interrupted by illness finds what they were really looking for by sitting still and watching, while elsewhere another eager vacationer discovers that no matter where you go, there you are.

We have stories from childhood—turning young minors into hardworking miners digging with spoon-sized shovels, sneaking out at night to do the daring thing and being caught by the gentle arm of the law, or other such nocturnal adventurers discovering at dawn the value of a good night's sleep. Another recalls getting pulled into a beating, nurturing questions decades later about camaraderie and fellowship.

We have stories of mistakes—a teacher not checking his ego or his assumptions about a student, others too confidently deciding "we can do this" when "we" doesn't have a clue, others learning about backpacking the trails along the path of overconfidence and no experience, or another learning that strings and snakes can look equally interesting to the young and naive.

We have stories about getting on the wrong bus to nowhere you'd want to go, and about traveling 400 miles to find the love that was waiting just for you to arrive, or about embracing the fact that some people have the special gift of loving everyone, or that a simple kindness from one so deeply admired can spark a first discovery of what love feels like.

We have stories about mothers and fathers, some absent or deficient, leaving enough space for a welcomed substitute, or others imprinting beliefs that would lead a daughter astray, and a father who happily, proudly welcomed yet another to a house already full, a mother who just wants five minutes to herself, or one who demands the impressionable child do a horrible deed and then keep it a secret forever.

Introduction

We have stories of love—a daughter struggling with anger at parents already dead; sisters expressing their mutual love through challenges, complaints, and compassion; the kindest people with the biggest hearts wanting to run away from their young families; a young couple facing fate's full-on assault of their plans to get married; and, a story of mature love giving itself more than only a second chance to find its footing.

"Your expectations will kill you," some have cautioned us. Perhaps, but only if we let them. Our wants, our hopes, our dreams are ours to have and to wrestle with. And in the bargains we make with our great expectations, we end up with stories to tell.

Enjoy these. •

Auld Lang Syne
by Jamie Cheshire

This is the infinite sound.

The sound of infinite height and infinite depth, of infinite distance and of the very close and the holy, and of remembering it.

This is the sound of all the conversations among all our hearts and all our angels all at one time together.

This is the sound of pausing longer before the finish, longer because we chose the pause and not because we've been delayed.

―――――――――

My first concussion came on the end of a thug boy's right arm one summer evening when I was in my mid-teens.

I didn't see it coming. I didn't know why I'd been cut away from the crowd at the diving show and I didn't know why I'd been muscled into such a secluded place. I didn't know why the pocky-faced weirdos on his left and right kept sneering and jabbing at me but it was clear the redhead in the middle was their king and I was going into a three-on-one fight.

No one really knew what had happened. Actually, no one knew anything had happened. There were no witnesses. No one knew how long I'd been lying where they'd left me in the woods before I was seen weaving home near twilight. And after drugs and drunkenness (both quite plausible) had been ruled out by the basic neurological exam I'd been given by Dr. Bender (yes, really his name) my parents were left with nothing but conjecture. So far as I know, they never heard what happened. Any of you who knew me then will understand why.

The aftermath story that emerged from the rumors and boasting was that there was a girl at the center of it. A Southside girl whose name, I think, was Lou Ann, had voiced some concern about whether or not I was giving her adequate attention. The red headed goon king, Lee Roy (yes, really his name), seemed to have his own ideas about who should've been giving Lou Ann attention.

In the few days it took for my vision to clear and my gait to stabilize, factions formed, threats and warnings of reprisals were exchanged and for a while it wasn't a good idea to go around without a friend.

In my life since then, I have never felt any kindness for Lee Roy or his pocky boys, or for Lou Ann for that matter. I dismissed them all and moved on.

In 1788, Robert Burns wrote our collective heart into Auld Lang Syne, which was meant to mark a precious and fleeting moment between two friends who knew their paths would soon separate. It quickly became the anthem of long yearning between all of us and everyone anyone loves. We all know this song. It's in our shared identity.

A choir can make this the sound of infinity, a choral miracle that calls you to look up and remember and even if you can't quite, you at least remember there is something to remember.

But it's a closed and individual remembering—even in a group. It's only natural that we feel it most for those we've known and loved or simply esteemed. It's natural that they dominate our awareness. Other people on other errands have other auld lang synes to comfort them.

But what if they don't?

Old Eben Flood, in Edwin Arlington Robinson's "Mr. Flood's Party," sang Auld Lang Syne to himself on the hill road home, alone with his jug. He had no other one to sing it to. He had outlived his generation and so, in the cold twilight above the town, he sang it to himself.

Could a time come when we need someone so much that even an old enemy will become a cherished friend with whom we can share a cup of kindness?

I hope not, not for any of us. But we know it happens.
And so, I hope we'll share it if given the chance.

Look here and know this. I want our friendship. I want the certainty of you. I want your life and your happiness present in the world. I want your kindnesses and your fondness in whatever direction you spread it. I want your forgiveness given freely. And I want your company, as impractical as that probably is, so that neither of us ever has to set our jug down by itself on the ground and sing only to our memories. I want your Auld Lang Syne to echo with mine across whatever distance, and I want your heart's thoughts and voice to join with mine and with those of the angels who are surely present here with us.

And as fervently as I want that for you and for us together, I think, now, I want it for Lee Roy and Lou Ann, too. At least I *want* to want it for them. Our acquaintance is old. Very old and mostly forgotten. So, true to the verse, it qualifies. And perhaps it doesn't matter now what its nature was then.

Happy New Year, everyone. I hope the year ahead finds you brave and steadfast, safe, intelligent and kind.

We'll drink that cup yet. •

Copyright 2025, Jamie Cheshire

Fascinated with every big and little thing, Jamie Cheshire has long been an avid student of design and structure. Having worked together with giants, he has had the extreme good fortune to practice his craft for most of the last four decades and has seen his work appear nationally and in several countries on three continents. He lives in Winston-Salem, North Carolina, with his beloved feral, hippie-chick wife, their three dogs and two cats. Deeply committed to the ordinary, he is constantly searching for a way to describe it.

[Editor's note: The author invites you to listen to Auld Lang Syne performed by The Choral Scholars of University College Dublin: Search by that title on *YouTube.com*]

Digging for Foo-Foo Dust
by Vicki Easterly

Cloverdale—the idyllic neighborhood where we grew up; the neighborhood of brick houses that all looked alike, as if God had squeezed them out with a giant pastry bag; the neighborhood where parents spanked each other's kids.

I was 10 one hot summer day. It was so hot we kids popped tar bubbles off the road and chewed them, so hot the beige grass pricked our bare feet as we played our made-up game of "swinging statues" in my front yard. When we grew tired of slinging each other around, the game was over. Anyway, it was boring after a while; besides it was time for everybody to go home for lunch.

I ordered them to come back with a spoon. They didn't know why, but I was the oldest, so if I said it, they knew there was a good reason. The gang was made up of my 4-year-old sister Debbie; Joe and Mark, the brothers next door; David from across the street; Teresa from up the street, and me.

After lunch we met at the ditch. Brown-eyed David was a bit shaken. He had almost been caught taking his mother's best spoon and would've received a hefty beating if he she'd seen him.

"What do we need these spoons for?" He asked.

"Because" I announced mysteriously, "we're going to dig for foo-foo dust!"

"Oh," said David, without questioning.

Chubby Teresa, sensing a thrill, piped up. "Let's do it! Wait! What's foo-foo dust?"

In a breathless voice, I explained that foo-foo dust was magic, it was deep in the ground, maybe a mile or so deep, and we couldn't give up digging until we found it.

"What's it look like?" asked Teresa.

"It's silver and sparkly, and when you sprinkle it on you, you can fly!"

Red-headed Debbie started to cry. "But I'm little. What if I can't dig enough?"

"We'll sprinkle a little left-over on you," I promised.

Joe was 8 and the oldest boy. He was a skinny, dark-haired kid. "Since I'm the oldest boy, can I dig first?" he asked.

"Sure, right after me," I instructed.

I was a scrawny brown-haired girl, who was shorter than Joe, but I reminded him that age trumped size, so I was the boss.

Six-year-old Mark was the spitting image of Joe and mimicked everything Joe did.

My troops awaited my directions. "Ok, everybody, hold your spoons up. When I say *Go*, start digging as fast as you can. OK, GO!" With that, spoons hit the dry dirt, but I had thought to bring a jug of water. When I poured the water onto the ground, it was clear one jug would not suffice, so I ordered everyone to run back home and bring their own jug to pour. Now we had mud—wonderful, wallow-worthy mud!

We tried to take turns, but the anticipation was too great. Besides, if we all dug at once, we would get to the foo-foo dust faster. We could be flying, we estimated, by suppertime.

After a while, Teresa's face turned pasty white. She ran behind the elm tree and threw up but came right back. Joe started coughing and wheezing until he worked up a full-blown asthma attack, but he would only sit on the shady porch long enough to catch his breath. Mark feigned his asthma attack and sat by Joe for its duration. Then they were back digging and slopping in the mud. I felt like I might pass out, but I never missed a scoop. We were tired, sick, sweaty, and dirty, but we were on a mission, and we persevered!

Debbie cried out, "I see something silver!" With that we dove our spoons more ferociously into the unforgiving ground. With unbearable excitement, we flung spoonfuls of dirt. Closer and closer we got to the magic foo-foo dust. Faster and faster, we dug.

Never had we had so great a task, and never had we had so much fun.

"Just a few more spoonfuls!" I blurted exuberantly. Boy, were we happy. Nothing could stop us now. *Nothing!*

Then mother came.

She jerked me up first, then Debbie. "You all get home," she told the others. "There's no such thing as foo-foo dust. You're just wearing yourselves out for nothing. Besides, you're ruining my ditch."

Poof! With those words our dream of foo-foo dust and flying was lost forever.

Sometimes I take a nostalgic drive through Cloverdale. The houses and ditch are still there. All that's different are the kids. I want to stop, roll down my window, and yell with the authority of my 10-year-old self, *DIG! DIG! FLY! FLY!*
I don't, of course, but how I wish I had a spoon and a jug with me every time. •

Copyright 2025, Vicki Easterly

Vicki Easterly, a retired disability advocate, lives in Frankfort, Kentucky. Several stories have appeared in prior PSPP anthologies. Her short story, "Hallie Holcomb's Hollow," published by the UK Carnegie Press, is based on a composite of her sweet clients. Her first book, *Miracles in the Mundane*, was selected for the annual Kentucky Book Festival. Calling on her days as a young mother, she is working on a children's book series. She continues to write memoirs and poetry. Vicki enjoys playing with her granddaughters and acting in community theatre. She vows to never grow up.

The (sorta kinda) Runaway
by Jo McElroy Senecal

The first time I tried to run away from myself was when my perfect, tiny baby boy was hyperventilating his face off, and I could barely hear the dinner pots clanging in my kitchen, and my husband was *finally* coming home, his 40-minute commute an eternity during "Witching Hour" of all babies everywhere, and all the love in the world for my fresh little family couldn't stand up to the crumbling mess I was becoming and as soon as my husband crept in the door, probably hoping for a scintilla of Norman Rockwell's water colored scene of cooing-baby-at-the-hearth-slurping-dimpled-fist while the smell of home-cooked fill-in-the-blank danced like fat motes and fairy dust, I all but thrusted the precious screaming fruit of our loins into his surprised, overcoat-encased arms, mumbled something wildly incoherent, and *ran*. And while I ran (apron around waist, hard-soled, boiled-wool slippers gripping toes and heels), I kept glancing back. The faster I ran and the more I looked back, the more I realized I was trying not to get away from my family (I already missed them) but I was trying to get away from *me*. Completely.

I remember thinking, *Who does this?* I don't deserve this good life. I am making a downright *mess* of things. Happy babies don't scream the color purple, meals have been made by humans for ten thousand years, and good people don't lose their voices from screaming silently for the past which had none of the things they (I'm the *they*) always hoped for and now have—right? I cried into the crisp evening air, and it cried back, enough that I felt okay again in my skin. Over the years I would continue to break my promise to try not running away from myself, to accept things, and self, as they are. And even, dare I say, to love who I am, how I mothered and made homes, and how perhaps it is not a terrible thing to want to run away, once in a while. But not in slippers.

The *last* time I tried to run away from myself was on a recent 800 km backpacking pilgrimage to Santiago de Compostela in Spain. With the same husband whose surprised arms caught the purple-faced pumpkin that was our crying infant a quarter-century ago, we followed ancient paths that would lead us to "The Field of Stars." Matt was supporting my quest to "let go" of recent, hard goodbyes from my volunteer pediatric palliative care work. It made sense at the time. I'd envisioned galloping on foot through the French Pyrenees, releasing some particularly rough losses into the French wind that would whip through the French trees, and by the time I'd reach Roncesvalles, where my husband would be waiting for me, I'd be a fresh new me! (*Cue the French horn.*)

I did indeed gallop on foot through the Pyrenees. And I did everything I'd set out to do. But bits and pieces of these particular deaths stuck to me, twigs in my heart. Weeks into the Camino, I would get an unrelated text from a nurse about a special nugget named Abby, now in a coma and in hospice.

I sent her mom a message to whisper my love over her girl. I continued to "carry" Abby with me. And as I did, hundreds of kids' voices jumped in and competed for my attention. My daily 6-hour, backpacked walk became even more packed.

This was not a bad thing. I have loved so many children over the years, besides my own cherished punks, and it's an honor to hold them lightly in my heart. But I needed room to root around there, to make sure I was not hoarding them. I always brag about having zero burn out and wanted to make sure I could keep my bragging rights. Yet to quiet their voices, I also had to quiet my others', and what better way to do that than to—try to—run away from myself?

My worries, insecurities, and criticisms, all front and center, pushed for release. My judgmental, unorganized, hyper sides clawed their way to the surface of me, and I walked as fast as I could, twenty pounds of stuff on my back, eight hundred pounds inside. I bolted up craggy hills and slid down ragged paths. I embraced strangers, butchered my Spanish, left a rock with written prayer and Abby's name at the base of Cruz de Ferro, sang with nuns, raced to Fisterra, "the end of the world," and threw my tear-stained burdens into the sea. And I came back home, still me.

And glad. •

Copyright 2025, Jo McElroy Senecal

A native fish-taco-loving San Diegan, Jo McElroy Senecal spent decades on the East Coast, blending professional stage and clown credits with various roles at magical powerhouses like The Hole in the Wall Gang Camp and The Big Apple Circus Clown Care. Her *New York Times* article hints at her passion for pediatric palliative care, which she continues to do along with adult hospice care

The (sorta kinda) Runaway

in Charleston, South Carolina. Jo writes with the inimitable Luna Six, her longtime fellow writers, and bows to the steady stream of spirits that yodel in her heart and soul.

Mom Won't Like It
by Edward von Koenigseck

At 7, I and my 14-year-old sister Jane took a walk near where we lived on Long Island. While passing a vacant, overgrown lot along the nearby shipping channel, we heard a soft meow coming from the reeds.

"Bring it here," Jane exclaimed, after I'd discovered the source.

Fetching the kitten, I passed it to her, saying, "Take it. But you know Mom won't let it in the house. She hates cats."

Jane smiled. "My God, it's beautiful—and helpless!" she said, snuggling the kitten. "I can change Mom's mind, you know." As the only girl, Jane was Mom's favorite child, and usually got her way. As we walked back to the house, Jane ordered, "Let me do the talking."

In our five-room rented apartment, Father was long gone, and Mom was stuck with five children. Once inside, Jane sang out, "Mom! I have a wonderful surprise!" Mom stared at Jane and the kitten.

"So, can it stay?" I asked. Mom said nothing but reluctantly relented to Jane's appeal. Still, we knew she was wondering, who would tend to it?

To seal the deal, Jane broke the quiet, volunteering. "I'll take care of it, Mom. Even get a box for a bed and everything." Jane named the kitten Sniffer. Mom never held it, and we boys had no interest. During the years Sniffer lived with us, Karl, the oldest, had quit school and joined the Navy and Peter joined the Air Force. Jane tended to Mom's needs as her health deteriorated. Skinner and I just played. Mom suffered in silence, resenting cat hairs everywhere. During her childhood, cats weren't pets or had names; they just caught barn rats.

After being discharged from the Navy, Karl bought a small five-room Cape Cod house. Mom, who decided what would stay and what wouldn't, seemed torn by some problem. A few weeks before our move she called me into the living room and said, "Bobby, we have a problem. You are the only one I can turn to." As the youngest sibling, I was still pretty naive.

"What's wrong, Mom?" I asked.

"The cat."

"What do you mean? Sniffer?"

"We've had cat hair ever since Jane brought that cat home. I'll not have it in our new house. We can't take it."

"If we leave her, she'll starve."

"I know. We have to kill it."

"*Kill her? Mom!*" I was shocked Mom would kill any animal even though she'd grown up on a farm. "How can you say that? Jane would never agree!"

"Jane can't ever know the truth. That cat will disappear, and it must always be a secret, our secret."

I was aghast. "*Why me? How?*"
"You have to drown it."

"*Oh, my God, Mom!* If Jane found out I did that, she would hate me forever, for killing the one thing she loves most! I can't, Mom."

"I'm sorry, Bobby. Cat hair everywhere bothers me, so not in our new home. You are the only one I trust."

"Drown her?" I asked still in shock. "In the tub?"

"No. Put it in a cardboard box with stones and drop it from the rowboat. And do it now. Jane's not home. Get an empty box. Rocks are by your boat. And get a rope."

Mom must have known what I was thinking, that I'd despise killing Sniffer.

"Yes, Jane will worry about what happened to her cat, but both of you will get over it. You will! Just remember, this secret is between us—just you and me, Bobby."

Gathering the box, rope, and oars, I went to the rowboat, threw the items in, then found some concrete chunks. Sniffer was home sitting on a window sill. I picked her up and returned to my boat. Holding her, I got into the boat, untied the attaching ropes, then pushed away so Sniffer couldn't jump out.

When in the channel by our house, I put three chunks of concrete in the box, then Sniffer. I gave her one last look, crying while choking out, "Forgive me, Sniffer. I have to do this." I closed the box flaps, then tied it shut while Sniffer meowed loudly. Momentarily holding it just above the water, I whispered, "Goodbye, Sniffer. Please forgive me." Before the box disappeared beneath the surface, I heard one last desperate pleading "meow."

I rowed home, slowly. Entering the living room, I said, "It's done," and went to my bedroom. A terrible lifelong secret had begun.

Would that a merciful God had let it end there. Two weeks later while walking the shoreline of the lot across the street, I saw a familiar shape. As I approached, to my horror I saw it was the body of a cat, or the remains of what had been a cat. Cardboard dissolves in water and internal gases floated Sniffer's body to the surface. The tide and wind pushed it ashore as surely as vengeance. Vacant eye sockets stared at me like a voice calling out, *Look at what you have done. Remember this forever.*

The sound of her last plaintive meow crying out has haunted me for over 70 years.

Forgive me, Sniffer. Please. •

Copyright 2025, Edward von Koenigseck

Edward von Koenigseck has a 40-year background in technical publications. He is the author of two books - a college textbook Technical Writing for Private Industry, and a memoir, Island Park, and has also published several short stories. His other activities have been providing 92 different lectures on biblical history for the nonprofit organization Shepherd's Center, and was hired to create the curriculum for and teach two semesters on technical writing for advanced English students at Florida Institute of Technology.

First Love
by David Lusk

I stood before the student body, parents, teachers, and administrators to deliver my campaign speech in a "new" blue shirt and khaki pants, fresh off a visit with my mother to the racks of the Goodwill store. Sunshine filled the auditorium. For inspiration, I had a sticker of Abraham Lincoln stuck to the upper lefthand corner of my notebook paper as I excitedly began reading my handwritten words, spelled out carefully in 5th grade cursive. My speech followed that of my opponent, the more popular and polished Don, the rival candidate from the other classroom. I was undaunted, though, because I had a secret power—a newfound ally. Between her and my stealthily placed Lincoln sticker, how could I fail?

Forever embedded in my memory is the first day I saw her, as she smiled at us, turned to the blackboard, then wrote her name—Miss Vail. Our new student teacher stood before us in stark contrast to the elderly Mrs. Hiatt, who often fell asleep at her desk with her mouth open while we silently read our assignments. For a shy, quiet, boy of 11, Miss Vail was a vision of loveliness. Her big, beautiful, smiling eyes, framed by long blonde hair, lit up the room. She was beautifully different. Her youthful face and arms were distinguished by a uniqueness like nothing I had ever seen. I later learned her radiance to be a skin condition called vitiligo. I was a preadolescent boy lost in a, heretofore, unknown love spell magnified by the magical thinking of childhood.

Riding my bike after school now became an imaginary free gallop toward the setting sun on an open plain with the prettiest of painted fillies. Those were days highlighted with sweet anticipation as I walked to school in the mornings, turning to shout and shoo my dog Sam back home. He too must have been curious about these mysterious feelings and thoughts that flooded my young heart and brain.

One day, the earth stood still for this love-struck boy, as I sat in my usual, purposefully inconspicuous seat in the back of the room. Her bright, brown eyes were fixed on me as she approached, stood over my desk, and said: "David, would you like to represent our class and run for president of the school"? The face of this 11-year-old boy gazing upwards at her natural, exquisitely Appaloosa-like beauty, and into her soulful eyes beamed in the affirmative, whether he stammered out any words or not.

I walked home that day, greeted by vigilant Sam, who puzzled with me over my assignment to write a campaign speech. *What could I possibly say that could persuade my peers to pick me over my popular opponent? More importantly, how could I win this election for Miss Vail and my class?* I remember wanting to write a speech that she would be proud of. With only 11 years of life experience, I had concerns but emboldened by the inspiring sound of her voice in my head, I forged ahead and gave my speech.

I did not win the election. Disappointing, but then came the harsher reality that Miss Vail would be leaving our classroom to go back to her college classes. I asked my mother if I could buy her a gift. We went to Roses Discount Department Store where, displayed in a glass case, I saw a small, "silver" jewelry box that opened to expose the soft, red-velvet compartment. After class, on her last day, after everyone had left, I made that slow walk to her desk and handed her my gift. Time stopped. She cried. Maybe she was touched by the gesture. Maybe she thought of herself as different for her appearance and had not imagined that someone else would see that difference as part of her beauty. *I was different too*, I thought. She had seen something inside me. Maybe we were both red velvet on the inside and nobody had ever told us that. I don't know.

On my way home that day, I sank into an unknown feeling I realize now was my first experience of heartache. Somewhere between her soft-spoken words of encouragement and her silent tears, she knew, better than I, that we would never see each other again. I simply felt alone, like never before.

I held onto my handwritten speech with the Abe Lincoln sticker throughout my grade school years. I came home from college to discover that all my missing childhood possessions, including my speech, had been "put in storage." That clean-out marked a symbolic end to my childhood.

All I really have missed, though, is that single piece of paper to remind me of my brief but glorious political career and the sweet gift of confidence in myself and the beauty we can find in another—a lesson that Miss Vail taught me 60 years ago. •

First Love

Copyright 2025, David Lusk

David Lusk is a retired consulting arborist/psychologist/writer living in Winston-Salem, North Carolina. He has previously written several articles for the Winston-Salem Journal and the trade publication, Tree Care Industry Magazine. He lives in a beech tree woodland with his wife Amy, their three adopted rescue shelter dogs, Jessie Girl, Captain Spaghetti Jack, Abbey Road and Maple Tree the cat. He is currently attempting to learn Japanese Sumi ink painting while under the constant, playful supervision of Jessie, Jack and Abbey. Often he retreats to the Pamlico Sound with the idea of learning to sail but happy to paint or play guitar in view of a marina full of boats and the occasional visit from a bald eagle he named Churchill.

Daddy's Girl
by Willow Noelle Groskreutz

I was 17. He was 26. I shouldn't have to say more, but he was in a relationship and considered a common-law spouse in the eyes of the state. The state also deemed 16 the age of consent. He looked into it after the fact.

I was bookish, shy, and convinced that society was a scam. The lush alley of my mind had grown dense and dark with thorns. But I was a good girl. Favorable grades, well-behaved. I was a daddy's girl, through and through. I would listen for the distinct rumble of his truck every afternoon to run out and greet him. We'd sit in the cab watching sunsets, talking as he drank beer, while I clung to every sentence like I did with my favorite stories. I sided with him during his divorce and became alienated from my mother.

The summer before my junior year, we moved to a new town. Three things happened. First, I lost both my cats and didn't know what to do with the stone lodged in my heart. Second, my dad's girlfriend moved in with us. She was eleven years younger than him, childless, and had her own ideas about how I should behave.

I started experimenting with cannabis to untether myself, but I was demonized overnight, mercilessly shamed, and accused of things I didn't do. One moment, I saw myself being treated as if I were my mother; the next, I had moved in with her and wore new school colors. At parting, my dad wished me good luck. We didn't speak for months. As I turned 17, my world flipped upside down.

Several weeks later, I started my first job, hostessing. A waiter asked, "Isn't your dad like a cult leader?" Admittedly, yes. Charismatic, vehemently antisocial. His word was my gospel. I didn't believe in the Father, I believed in *my* father.

Now he was all but invisible while I was alone like a doe lost in the woods. Then, the brush parted, and I was approached by a caramel coyote, slipping out of a convertible Camaro, and he asked to befriend me.

I was pretty but also pretty weird, and therefore never had much traction with boys my age. But in his words, I was a mythical creature. He moved quickly, never missing an opportunity to indulge his earthly pleasures. We shared more moons than suns because, as a dancer, his partner worked nights. We'd sit in their bedroom, smoking blunts while he talked, and I listened. Though his gregarious personality contradicted my father's, he preached the same.

I believed him when he said he loved me. I was willing to look past his way of saying nearly nothing when answering serious questions or by meeting my hesitation with persistence. I abandoned whatever I was doing to see him after weeks of silence even after he moved away to follow his latest hustle. Missing him was my excuse for the hollow shell my body had become.

At parting, he encouraged me to explore other men, as though he were setting me free. I said okay, wishing someone would claim me like a gem from the sea. But, by now, he lived in my mind, and I grabbed at him like coals from a fire in the freezing cold.

Meanwhile, loneliness assaulted me, finally breaking through like repeated blows on a frozen lake. I tried to move on, engage my interests, meet new people, but then my phone displayed his name. The porch light revealed his face. Each time, there was never any closure, just him undoing his pants without asking and disappearing. Once, he commented he'd always come to see me, even if I were married. I remember thinking, *what the fuck?*

All this time, I ignored the feeling that I wasn't enough of something, like he'd rather me be in crop tops than flannel, bubbly and boisterous than pensive and pessimistic. The simmering suspicion that I was a cliche boiled over. I was the other woman: a little girl with daddy issues.

It's taken nine years to dissect the mites he left in me and see that I was not deficient; he was not right for me. Understanding the source of my attraction prevented me from perpetually falling for men who fed on vulnerability, and I would recognize that genuine love comes without coercion. The obstacles preventing my fairy tale with him revealed themselves as safety blockades leading me towards the moment I would raise my hand and say, *thank god I didn't get what I thought I wanted.* •

Copyright 2025, Willow Noelle Groskreutz

Willow Noelle Groskreutz is a creative writer based in Mooresville, North Carolina. In 2023, she self-published *Mundane Magic*, a collection of Southern-inspired lyric essays about finding wonder in everyday places. Willow is a recipient of the 2025 Artist Support Grant from the North Carolina Arts Council and looks forward to furthering her writing career.

The Recliner
by Anne Anthony

Friday morning, I arrive at my sister's assisted living facility to dismantle her old recliner. Mary is waiting in her wheelchair on the front porch.

"I've been waiting since 7." She's quick to find fault, like Dad.

"Told you I'd be here at 8." I bend to kiss her cheek.

"The new recliner is already delivered. It's brown, not maroon, like the photo you sent."

"Enjoy the morning sun while I set it up," I say and head inside.

Mary took ownership of Dad's old recliner after he died. In his final years, he developed a habit of rubbing his fingertips on the armrests. I run mine across those well-worn patterns before dismantling the recliner. The back pulls out easily with a tug and separates. Beneath it, I discover discarded items—dusty magazines, used tissues, and boxes saved from Christmas. It's July.

Getting a new recliner with a remote was my sister's idea to alleviate the spasms she feels stretching over the armrest to the manual controls. Her whole body experiences ripples of confused nerve firings since birth. Will she miss the traces of Dad— the red stain where an aide spilled cough medicine, two colorless indentations where his slippers rubbed off the footrest fabric, and those circles which she now traces, too?

After finishing, I return to her, now napping in the sun, touch her hand lightly to wake her, and crouch to eye level.

"You know, how you hate change?"

"Yea, I know."

"Give the new recliner a chance?"

I take a deep breath, wheel her back, and navigate a three-point turn so she may face the new recliner.

"That color is the same shade as Dad's eyes," she says, leaning forward to feel the fabric. "And soft. Like Dusty." Hope rises at the mention of her dead cat, gone 14 years.

She hoists herself up, her legs unsteady, before turning to sit. The recliner teeters forward.

"*It'srockingIcan'tkeepsteadyWhydidyougetmearockerI'mgoingtofall!This- won'twork!*"

As she hollers, I remind myself: *she can hardly hear, remember, since birth? Not because she's mad.* The recliner didn't move in the showroom, I tell her, but now, I picture it there leaning up against another. I check the tag. Rocker. Special-ordered upholstery. No returns. Mary can't handle a rocker; she's quick to startle and falls easily—once when a dog barked, again when an aide fixed her blouse, and a third during a social hour when she attempted to dance.

"It's hard to get into." She tries scooching back, then glances at the clock. "It's lunchtime. I'll try later."

The stare-off begins. Puss-faces, Mom called us. A game of chicken, I think. Seven years older, decibels louder, she always won. Today is no exception. She knows, I know, that mealtime breaks the day's monotony.

"Fine."

It takes five minutes to wheel her to the dining room; she's quiet for a change, giving me time to think about the recliner she doesn't love. I keep her company while she eats.

"Thank you for all you've done to get the new recliner," she says, astutely reading my silence. Sometimes, her flip of moods feels like gaslighting.

"Your complaints are exhausting."

"I wasn't complaining. I was surprised."

"Sometimes *how* you say something sounds like complaints."

"I wasn't complaining," she mumbles, poking at her fishcake.

Before leaving, I ask her to try the recliner for one night.

Returning home, I uncork a bottle of Chardonnay. Yes, it's two o'clock. Yes, I never ate lunch. And yes, I drop into the familiar hole of failure which goes deeper than the recliner. It's tied to my father, *our father*, who has been dead for years. I chase his approval through my sister. Is there a psychiatric term? *Unresolved Daddy-Issues by Proxy?*

Saturday morning, I wake dreaming about my sister dying. I'm surprised my pillow is damp. Her email arrived overnight.

I didn't sleep good last night. The worst night and day so far.

Give it another night.

Sunday morning, Mary sends her decision.

I want my old recliner back.

The Recliner

Ok.

Swapping recliners takes less than 20 minutes. Mary brightens and settles in. I flash to the memory of Dad in this recliner answering my question asked years before.

"What's going to happen after you're gone, after you've spoiled her, after always giving in?"

"She'll be your problem then," he'd said, with a shameless grin.

My husband and I drag the non-returnable recliner into our house. I sink into its gentle cushion, press the remote to recline, and close my eyes.

Monday, I'm rocking in the new recliner reading email. Mary thanks me for the great night's sleep in her old recliner. Her email continues…*My computer isn't working right; I might need a new one.*

I stop rocking. Call out to my husband, making breakfast. "Add another bottle of Chardonnay to the grocery list!" •

Copyright 2025, Anne Anthony

Anne Anthony tends to carry on conversations with characters inside her head when writing her stories. A few years back, she stopped shushing them, agreed to tell their stories, and they've all been happy ever since. She lives and writes in North Carolina. Her recent publications include *Bull, Gooseberry Pie Lit Magazine, Flash Boulevard, Flash Fiction Magazine,* and elsewhere. Her micro-fiction, "It's a Mother Thing," was nominated for Best Microfiction 2024 by *Cleaver Magazine*. She is a senior editor and art director for the online literary journal, *Does It Have Pockets*. Find more of Anne's writing at https://linktr.ee/anchalastudio.

Love Finds a Way
by Barbara Reese Yager

Breeders of Airedale Terriers will sometimes relinquish older puppies, the ones not so cute or sellable. As the lead person for the southeastern U.S. rescue group for Airedale Terriers, I hand-picked the families trusted to love these offered canine companions.

I had on hand a mother and two 6-month-old puppies from a breeder. The pups were intelligent, playful, and loyal – all Airedale Terrier attributes. I recognized brilliance. So, who was worthy of these creatures?

A volunteer from our sister group in Maryland asked to place the male with a family. They lived outside LaPlata surrounded by acres of woodland. She vouched for them personally. I agreed, though now it was complicated for me, having kept the pups for a while. Blue sat on my foot, leaned back, and looked up with loving eyes. He cautiously crawled his long frame onto the king-size bed. He would sit at the back door when I left for work, and he was there when I returned. Could I really place him?

"Transport Saturday" came. Blue hopped onto the back seat, and we drove north from my farm through South Carolina for the transfer to our Raleigh volunteer, Christina, who would take Blue on to Maryland. Blue rode contentedly. He was safe.

At the handoff, Christina looked at Blue, then to me and asked, "How can you give him up? He seems devoted to you."

"I know, but it's my job with the rescue group, Christina. Could I really keep a promised dog?" I handed over his leash.

Blue hesitated to go with Christina; he kept looking back. After they pulled away, I sat in my car and cried. I had a long, sad drive home alone as Christina drove Blue on to Maryland.

I almost always get a thank you call from the adopters as soon as they get their new dog. Hearing nothing by Sunday afternoon, I panicked and called. The father answered.

"Oh. Yeah. I have bad news about that. I didn't want to call you. Blue ran away on Saturday; his first time out. We loosened his collar, and he backed out coming up the deck stairs. He's out in the woods—somewhere."

"He also answers to Boo-Boo," I blurted out, wanting to be helpful to their recovery efforts.

"Yeah. We could see him, but he wouldn't come. He's gone." He went on, "You will understand that we have to move on. Our children can't be in a state of worry."

No, I did not understand. Blue was lost—and 400 miles from the one who loved him. What idiot loosens a new dog's collar? Who searches for a lost dog only one day? How could they give up on a dog like Blue?

The volunteers of my rescue group gave me some real-world dog trapping advice. One discouraged me from attempting to get Blue back, said I would never see him again. I simply could not abandon him.

Christina and I completed our work duties and then organized the supplies for our search party. We drove to Maryland. At dawn, I walked in the woods where Blue was first lost. As far as I could see, a carpet of brown and black leaves provided perfect Airedale camouflage. Discouraging. Intuitively Christina drove to the tiny country store at the crossroads five miles south to inquire. "Yes," said the store owner. She had fed a black and tan dog one night from the lane yonder.

That country lane was a long crescent of houses and farms. At one end, we parked the car and a pile of my smelly socks to attract Blue. Christina wore one of my jackets as a scent magnet. We brought out Baylee, my girl Airedale, as a lure. As we walked the crescent, we spooned out cat food in a path toward our car. Smelly food attracts a hungry dog. We searched and planned to search into the night between the lane and the country store. We were prepared to search for five days.

We reached the last farm at the end of the crescent and stood still. It was early morning. Dew was still on the grass. Would Blue even be awake? In the woods behind the stone house, I could hear dogs, but I didn't recognize his bark. Could he be down that dirt lane? I wanted to go but I didn't want to be shot walking on private property. I called, "Boo-Boo," again, staring hard down the lane.

In an instant, Blue was 50 feet away. *Was I hallucinating?*

Love Finds a Way

He went to Christina; he was on my scent. She knelt and got the slip-leash ready, but he backed away. I was on my knees, crying out, "Boo-Boo!" He came at a galloping romp. He knocked me down, licking away my tears of joy. Tears of doubt. Tears of relief.

Four days. Four hundred miles. A lost dog waiting for one person. •

Copyright 2025, Barbara Reese Yager

Barbara Reese Yager, a lifelong dog rescuer, writes fiction and nonfiction. She is president of the Charlotte Writers Club and a member of the North Carolina Writers Network and the South Carolina Writers Association. Her nonfiction work had appeared in previous anthologies of the Personal Story Publishing Project. She lives on a farm with her husband, four horses, five dogs, and a barn cat. Find more of Barbara's writing at *waggintailfarm.com*

Yeses
by Richard L. Davis

Two bright-eyed "Yeses!" greeted me one evening at the dinner table, where all of life's best decisions should be made. Earlier that day the Pentagon had offered me a job as an air attaché, a uniformed diplomat, at the U.S. Embassy in Kinshasa, Zaire, once the Belgian Congo. I would represent the U.S. Air Force Chief of Staff to his counterpart in a foreign capital. It was an ancient dream and a great opportunity for me, a career officer; but what would Myra and Diane, my wife and youngest daughter, think about living for two years in central Africa?

Their eager "yeses" were, if anything, even more enthusiastic than mine. We had already traveled globally together, from Asia to Europe. Myra, a travel-addicted professional ice skater, longed to see more countries. And Diane yearned to see the jungles and exotic animals of the continent. So, I signed us all up without further hesitation.

Myra and I first trained together for a year as an attaché couple, learning French, how to survive in a foreign environment, how to place knives and forks for formal dinners—all very genteel—and very exciting. Equally eager for adventure, Diane would delay college for a year to join us.

By mid-August 1991, we were on our way. We landed in a country with a population divided into two worlds. Most (30 million people) walked barefoot on dirt roads and lived in mud shacks with blankets for doors. The other, a rapacious ruling clique of 15,000, headed by a guy who called himself Mobutu Sese Seko Kuku Ngbendu Wa Za Banga, lived within lush, high-walled compounds with fine wines and regular trips to Europe. President Reagan once called Mobutu "a Great Friend of Freedom." But his ostentatious name in his native Lingala meant, "Rooster who leaves no hen intact." That said it all. Mobutu, a 1960s-era creature of the CIA, had become a billionaire while his people dealt with 8,000 percent annual inflation. They faced a situation that could not last. For us, it lasted four weeks.

A great leader often motivates his followers with optimistic visions and martial metaphors. However, Mobutu preferred to motivate with money, buying off his minions by pitting one faction against another. If his state police, aka Civil Guard, went on strike, he could always pay his elite Presidential Division enough raw cash to restore order. And vice versa.

Now, however, galloping inflation meant money no longer worked. On September 23, 1991, both the Guard and the Division rioted. The general population soon joined, and the whole country collapsed. Crowds swarmed through Kinshasa. Gunfire could be heard everywhere. Soldiers seized the airport and its customs office. Rioters looted stores and homes. And … people died—hundreds of Zairians, numerous Belgian and Lebanese businessmen, even the French ambassador. Fortunately, Americans were not targeted, but rioters twice marched on the American Embassy, demanding that Mobutu be ousted.

Diane and I were stuck in town when it started. Myra, still at our home on a hillside outside of town, watched from the veranda as columns of smoke marked the rioters' progress through the city. That sinking feeling affected all three of us. Our State Department soon ordered all Americans evacuated and reduced embassy staff from 1,000 down to 35 personnel, including me. On September 27, I watched my two beloved girls head off to another country and a world away. It would be months before I would see them again.

After they left, I worked with our Belgian and French allies to orchestrate the evacuation of another 26,000 people, representing 38 countries. Suffering no evacuee casualties, we did it in less than two weeks from a country the size of the eastern U.S. But they left behind a ghostly legacy.

I stayed in-country most of the following year, senses overwhelmed by what I saw. Here, an unclaimed body lay in a gutter, decapitated and bloated. There, a cleaned human skull grinned from atop a marble mileage marker. The charm had gone out of the place.

It seemed futile to buck these chaotic, insoluble forces buffeting Zaire. Yet even though our initial plans had failed, our hopes remained undiminished. Diane spoke for all three of us when she later wrote in her journal:
> "Africa was hard to explain, but it almost seemed as if my heart was there, like I'd come home. So beautiful ... Problems, yes, but to send everyone back to the U.S.? We didn't have a choice. If we had, I would've stayed, Myra, too.

Yeses

"During this whole thing, I was much less than thrilled. But I didn't want to leave and still see no reason for us to be evacuated.

"I want to go back!"

Yes. •

Afterword
Colonel Rick Davis remained in Zaire through spring 1992, but Myra and Diane never did "go back," as Diane wished. The U.S. and Belgian governments later recognized Rick for his work during the evacuations, and the Air Force gave him and Myra another attaché assignment to India. Meanwhile, Mobutu was ousted, finally, in 1997 and died the same year.

Pronunciation Gazetteer
For the language challenged, Mobutu's name, Mobutu Sese Seko Kuku Ngbendu Wa Za Banga, is pronounced:
Moe-BOO-two SAY-say SAY-koh KOO-koo ing-BEN-doo Wah Zah BAHN-gah …
Try it out loud three times fast. Good luck.

Copyright 2025, Richard L. Davis

Richard ("Rick") Davis retired from the Air Force in 1998 and lives in Elk Grove, California. He has an extensive professional writing history, including some non-fiction material published over the past 40 years. To transition to fiction, he studied with Amherst Writers & Artists and published his first novella in 2014. "Yeses" marks Rick's fourth contribution to Personal Story Publishing Project anthologies.

Vacation
by Eloise Currie

Dawn spreads over the sky as I step onto the balcony and into the briny ocean breeze, the sun a cheerful pink-red coin on the horizon. I have anticipated these days, a full weekend, for ten years. I let the rising heat wrap around me for a lovely twenty minutes before going out to wade in warm water that turns into a foamy froth around my feet.

Walking the unpopulated beach, I squeeze sand between my toes, taking in salty, fish-tasting air, the sun on my shoulders and neck unknotting tension built up over two decades of worrying and caring—first, years of constant visits to Dad in the Alzheimer's facility, then moving Mom into my house when heart failure set in. A nurse stayed with her during the day, and I took over when I got home from work. Constantly on the alert for the sound of her frequent falls or calls for help, I had no downtime. Permanent exhaustion set in.

The sun sends a streak of light across the water. Gulls march smartly through the sand or fly overhead in formation. Shells wash up, shiny-clean. Waves suck sand from under my feet, throwing me off balance. I have an uneasy moment of vertigo.

The pier, a planned destination, is hazy in the distance. I remember walking its hot, grey-black boards, leaning over the rail, and watching water swirl between massive, barnacle-covered wood pilings. It will be comforting. But it is not the old familiar pier I see; the friendly wooden thing that shifted and groaned with the waves is gone, replaced by a concrete version. The change is unnerving.

Standing on rough concrete, I lean on the rail and watch as the beach shifts from peaceful to unexpectedly overpopulated, this once-quiet place now crowded with people lugging coolers, umbrellas, radios, and chairs, all elbowing for space. No one is a minimalist anymore, sitting on the sand with only a towel and book; now, half an hour is required to get established for the day. People huddle under umbrellas, eating, complaining of sand in bathing suits, listening to competing music that drowns out calming ocean sounds. I pick my way through the crowd to the water to bounce in warm waves. This used to be relaxing but now fails to rid the brain of thoughts I had vowed I would leave at home.

Decisions suddenly hit hard and fast—*do what, go where? Sit on balcony, read book, stare at the water?* What to do if there is no necessary thing to be done? After years of work and caregiving, every moment spoken for, maneuvering through an empty day is an unsettling mystery.

The pool is an option. I take a chaise and watch a group of women opposite me. They obviously have no intention of getting wet; jewelry and makeup give them away. All laugh, ordering rounds of multicolored cocktails with umbrellas or fruit on a frilled toothpick. Drink in hand, one wobbles to her feet, sliding into high-heeled sandals, tottering into furniture, giggling. Their conversation, clearly audible, is superficial. But something about them registers—they know how to live in the moment.

The waiter brings the frilly-drinks menu. I hand it back and order wine.

Alcohol-fueled, I have the wherewithal to walk to the antique shop across the street. Filled with miscellaneous castoffs, the scent of age is pervasive. Tourists snap up treasures, not unlike the contents of my mother's house which I will soon be clearing out. I push that thought away. Finding the shop suddenly claustrophobic, I escape.

Mechanically, I return to the pool and swim laps, the water warm and silky. I relax slightly with fortification from a second glass of wine; I have sunk to the point that only chemicals and exertion can tamp down shaky nerves. Lying on a chaise, brain numb and unrefreshed, I am confused by the unexpected difficulties of the day—of what to do next with an empty schedule in this now-unfamiliar place.

A niggling thought comes—I have done everything I looked forward to. I try to push it away, but it is stubborn. I have seen the sun rise and set, felt heat, swam, wandered. But I have failed to snatch and hold on to peace. I cannot mentally decompress; I consider tomorrow—a once-anticipated stretch of time I now view with dread.

Post-sunset, I order room service and, wine-assisted, mechanically begin aggregating things, pushing them into the suitcase.

Vacation

Shaken, I realize this is not the place I need; the brain calls for home. I can be there tomorrow by noon, safe again with my cats, making progress on what needs doing. I begin to appreciate the peace I find in routine.

But I am jolted by the realization that routines—like places—shift, change. What then? •

Copyright 2025, Eloise Currie

Eloise Currie lives in Raleigh, North Carolina. This is her second piece accepted by the Personal Story Publishing Project. She has kept a journal for thirty years and uses it as material for short stories and nonfiction. She enjoys editing and has edited books as well as short stories.

Take the Girls Seriously
by Mary Clements Fisher

Running up the ramp to the cafeteria, I stumbled when a voice hit my back like a pellet gun. "Stop. Right now." I whipped around to see Mr. Stevens, one of our school counselors, striding toward me. "Where do you think you're going, young lady?" His booming timbre rattled the glass in the windows. Without hesitation I flashed my back off eyes at him before I grinned. Both big mistakes.

I passed his office on my way to my humanities class every day, but in a high school with 4,400 students and 150 teachers running through the hallways between class periods, I became a blur to him. Today I wore a short skirt, a red cashmere sweater, and my red flats. Another big mistake—like driving a red sports car too fast in the school zone.

"You should be in class. Where's your pass?" He laid his hand on my shoulder and closed the space between us. I shuddered. Bushy eyebrows, stale breath, hairy forearms, he growled, "Where is it?"

Keeping my voice low and steady to sound older, I tossed him a you're-making-a-big-mistake smile, eyebrow cocked. "I don't need a pass. I'm a teacher here. I'm on my way to the lunchroom and I'm late."

He laughed at me. "Oh, little sister, that's enough out of you." His jaw muscles flexed. He ground his teeth, and I locked my jaw. I could teach this guy a lesson: Don't judge a book by its cover.

His hand clamped onto my shoulder. "Ouch." I yanked my arm to break his hold. He squeezed tighter. When a bully grabbed me in grade school, I kneed him and ran all the way home, overkill in this instance, but not unwarranted. In junior high, a basketball coach slapped us girls on the bottom with a cheery "Good work." I told him to cut it out. He kept doing it anyway. I dropped out of basketball before high school.
I loved basketball.

I sighed and contemplated my next best move with Mr. Stevens: Try to persuade him or let this play out. His nostrils flared and his cheeks flamed. "You're a sassy one, aren't you?" Sassy isn't how I'd frame the comment caught in my throat.

"I'm telling you, I'm a teacher." I stared into his bloodshot eyes with every ounce of sincerity I could muster. He clutched my arm and twirled me around. My chin went up and my back went stiff.

"We're going to the dean's office."

My anger bubbled over. "You'll be sorry" slipped from my lips.

He snorted and pressed his thumb deeper above my collar bone. A bruise would blossom there soon. How did this guy keep his counseling job? He missed the memo about not touching students, ever. His crooked smile gave me the creeps.

A couple hundred yards to the dean's offices was more than I could bear. I balked after 20 steps. The dean's never encountered me before. Besides, I overheard two of the deans yesterday teasing girls pressed against their lockers by boys twice the girls' size. They might declare no harm done and laugh this off. "How about a stop at the principal's office? It's closer."

He wavered. "I don't know what you're up to but okay. Let's say hi to Mr. Vallicelli. He won't like your attitude." My attitude? His attitude registered Cro-Magnon on the unenlightened scale.

When we walked past the teachers' mailboxes, I came close to saying, you might want to unhand me now but at this point, this guy had made up his mind. So had I. I wanted him to suffer.

The fool didn't let go. We turned into the administrative office. Ms. Cavenaugh, the administrative assistant, stared at his hand gripping my shoulder, cocked her eyebrow, and called out, "Why, hello, Mr. Stevens and Mrs. Fisher! What can I do for you two?"

His hand slid off my shoulder. I swallowed my I told you. Flushed, he muttered into his chest, "Sorry. . . hmmm, I've kept Mrs. Fisher from her lunch too long," and scuttered out the door to leave Ms. Cavenaugh perplexed and me vexed.

I never reported the pain Mr. Stevens inflicted on me. I didn't trust the system then. I regret that. The following week all teachers and other staff at Proviso West High School wore

Take the Girls Seriously

lanyards with names and department printed in 16-point type. Mr. Stevens kept his job. My bruises faded. His humiliation did not. Whenever we met in the halls, I gave him a drop-dead stare. He lowered his chin and cleared his throat like something was stuck in his craw. I retired my pencil skirt—senior boys sometimes mistook me for a classmate—but I often wore my red sweater and shoes to celebrate one small victory for young women. •

Copyright 2025, Mary Clements Fisher

Mary Clements Fisher celebrates her student and writer status in Northern California. Her writing unearths buried mad, muddled, and magical moments. She's published in *Quail Belle Magazine*, *Adanna Journal*, *Prometheus Dreaming Journal*, *The Closed Eye Open*, *Capsule Stories*, *They Call Us Magazine*, Nailpolish Stories, and several Personal Story Publishing Project books. Join her @maryfisherwrites and https://maryfisherwrites.squarespace.com/

Behind Lace Curtains
by Valerie J. Macon

The sky hung heavy with thick, snowy clouds. Alice, my next-door neighbor, pulled her lace curtains aside and peaked out her kitchen window. Her two chocolate labs, who she lovingly calls *The Girls*, paced nervously in the backyard pen. "*The Girls* are cold. Mommy is going to let them in," she called out to her 4-year-old daughter, Christie, who was snuggled in an overstuffed chair watching *Sesame Street*. Leaving the door ajar, she darted out in her slippers and bathrobe to the pen at the back of the small yard. She unhinged the gate, and the shivering labs raced ahead of her to the back door.

Alice arrived at the door a few steps behind the labs, but found the door closed. She turned the doorknob. It was locked. Cupping her hands, she peeked through the curtains. Inside, she saw Christie in the pantry on her tiptoes reaching for a bag of cookies. Shivering, Alice rapped on the door and called out to her, "Open the door, Darling! Mommy and *The Girls* are cold." Hugging the bag of *Oreos*, Christie grinned at her mother's face in the window as she skipped past the door. Alice watched through the glass as her daughter climbed back into her tv chair and buried her face in the bag of cookies.

Alice dashed around to the front of the house, *The Girls* at her heels. She tried the front door. It, too, was locked. Now, snowflakes the size of quarters began drifting down from the gray sky. Alice hobbled over shrubbery skirting the house and positioned herself at the den window with a clear view of Christie perched in the chair. Pressing her nose to the pane, she knocked on the glass calling out to her daughter to open the door. Christie, her mouth ringed in chocolate, licked the white cream from a split *Oreo*. She smiled at her mother, holding up the two halves of the cookie.

A chill rippled through Alice from her uncombed hair to her slippered feet. Her hands were turning numb, and her feet were beginning to feel like icy stumps. She rapped on the window. "Mommy is cold, open the door!" she pleaded. Christie slid out of the chair, leaving a scatter of brown crumbs on the seat. She appeared at the window. Pushing the lace curtains aside, she smiled, her teeth brown with chocolate. She held up the bag of *Oreos*. "I'm eating cookies!" she said.

Frantic, Alice scrambled to check the garage door. It, too, was locked. The dogs, sensing a crisis, zipped around the yard in a frenzy. Alice darted from window to window, climbing through snow-dusted bushes, pushing up on icy window frames, her hands stiff with cold. "Christie!" she hollered through chattering teeth. "Let me in!" Christie, stuffed with *Oreos*, followed her mother from window to window, placing rows of the cream-filled cookies in straight lines on each sill.

Desperate, Alice raced across the snow-glazed yard to use my phone. After several rings, Christie answered, "Hello, I'm eating cookies," she reported. "Christie, this is Mommy, open the door. It's okay that you're enjoying cookies, I'm not mad, I'm just cold . . . *The Girls* are cold, we want to come in, please open the door!"

"No!" said Christie, before she hung up the phone. Christy peaked from behind the curtains as neighbors, hearing the ruckus, gathered in the yard. They began to craft plots and toss ideas as the snow swirled around them. One neighbor brought over Christie's favorite kitten, offering him up at the window to coax her out of the house. Another slid her library card along the doorjamb trying to pop the lock. Another got a crowbar and tried to jimmy a window open.

Suddenly, the front door began to creak open, just a sliver. Activity came to a stop. A hush fell over the group. All eyes fixed on the gray front door. A small figure stood in the doorframe, her pale face smeared with brown cookie, her belly bulging under her Carter pants. An empty cookie bag dangled from her fingertips then dropped to the ground. Haltingly, Christie walked to her mother and circled Alice's shivering body with her embrace. She began to retch and heave, then hurled a volume of undigested *Oreos* over her mother's snow-crusted robe and slippers.

Drawn to the welcoming warmth escaping the house, *The Girls* zipped through the crowd. With frenzied exhilaration they rushed side by side through the open door. In a clumsy tangle, they managed to bump the door shut behind them.

Soon, two chocolate faces peaked out from behind lace curtains. •

Copyright 2025, Valerie J. Macon

Valerie J. Macon, a writer residing in Fuquay-Varina, North Carolina, finds poetry and prose woven into the fabric of everyday life.
With six poetry collections to her name (*Shelf Life*, *Sleeping Rough*, *A String of Black Pearls*, *The Shape of Today*, *Page Turner*, and *Chasing After the Wind*), her work has found expression in a variety of forms from print to podcasts. Currently, she is working on a memoir and is a feature writer for Suburban Living Magazine.

A Landlubber's Tale
by Arlene Mandell

He was a captain on the high seas. I was a landlubber, unequivocally rooted on *terra firma*. We met at a dinner-dance. I liked him, he liked me. We needed to find common ground.

Determined to share his love of the watery world, he invited me for an introductory afternoon of sailing. His sunny apartment in North Miami opened onto a dock housing his Dolphin 24-ft. sailboat. We motored along the narrow canal that opened into Biscayne Bay, a huge body of water surrounded by metropolitan Miami. Then, unfurling the sails, he stayed close to the shoreline, lined with magazine-cover homes and manicured lawns.

This excursion remained delightful until the trip home when we ran aground on a sandbar in the canal. It would take three or four hours for the tide to roll in and float us free, but we would have to wait it out. Was this the sailor's equivalent of a car running out of gas on a first date? *Hmm...clever*, I thought.

Killing time in the balmy, late-afternoon air, we played cards, chit-chatted, and devoured the snacks. He then beguiled me with the story of his harrowing experience on the U.S. Coast Guard cutter *Bibb*. Caught in a monstrous storm of high winds and heavy seas, the *Bibb* had rolled to a perilous angle approaching 60 degrees. His crucial task was to prevent the engines from over-speeding during the ship's violent pitching. Captivated, I was not in a hurry to get back. I liked being stuck with the guy.

The following week, we ventured farther out into Biscayne Bay. Working the sails, using the wind, while precariously perched on the rim of the gunnel, he shouted in exultation as we zigged and zagged, causing the boat to "heel" from one side to the other. Obsessing over which side to jump off if we capsized, I could not share his joy but said nothing.

One idyllic Florida morning, he suggested lunch at a dockside restaurant on the Intracoastal Waterway (ICW). We would motor there, have lunch, and return home. The ICW—a congested mass of two-way traffic coming and going, entering and exiting, whizzing crosswise—was chaotic but par for the course to a seasoned boater. Lunch was a relief from the hubbub, ending too soon for my liking.

Leaving for the trip home, we cast off, sailing with motor-assist, as the wind was not favorable. Without warning, the engine quit while approaching a bascule drawbridge. Not having enough speed to clear the bridge, we quickly turned—under sail—toward a nearby island. We dropped anchor there, but he could not get the engine going again.

He devised a plan to sail through the bridge by gaining speed upon approach and having the bridge open just in time. It would work if the bridge tender would open the bridge "on demand." A call on marine radio found the bridge tender cooperative. With the captain's signal, and bridge tender's reply, we raised anchor and sailed back into the stream of ICW traffic, making it through the bridge and all the way back to our slip at the dock. Emotions drained, I was, nevertheless, taken with his coolheadedness in the face of danger, so opposite my "oh-my-god-the-sky-is-falling" nature. He had the heart of a captain. I needed that, but sailing was not for me. I bailed out.

Taking a different tack at enjoying the bay, we looked at a 17-ft. Mako powerboat which came with a bucket and towel. Not sure what the towel was for, but too embarrassed to ask, he bought the boat anyway. However, sitting ingloriously on a bucket in the middle of Biscayne Bay responding to nature's call did not work for me. I bailed out a second time.

Next was an Ocean Reef 26-footer. It was sea-kindly and looked like a little tugboat, complete with a cozy cabin, where I could hide out. I thought that would work until the boat kept "snaprolling"—abruptly flinging everything around inside the cabin, including me. Decrying the snap rolls, I bailed out for the third time.

Three strikes, you're out! What next?

"How do you feel about camping?" he asked as we visited a nearby storage unit. He rolled up the door to unveil an Xplorer 22-ft. camper he drove on trips to the Great Smoky Mountains. "Wanna take a ride?" he tempted. Yes, I did—in a miniature home on wheels! I took to it right away—like a duck to water, so to speak.

A Landlubber's Tale

Years later, weary of city life and needing a sea change, we relocated to the High Country of Western North Carolina, opening a glorious world of mountains and forests to explore and exult in—together. He sold the sailboat, powerboat, and tugboat, but held on to the girl. Campgrounds became our common ground, and key in our lives to this day.

I still like being stuck with the guy.•

Copyright 2025, Arlene Mandell

Arlene Mandell is an artist living in Linville, North Carolina, proudly celebrating her 12th year at Carlton Gallery in Banner Elk. (carlton-gallery.com/arlene-mandell). A native New Yorker, relocating to the Blue Ridge Mountains with Captain Dan ignited a passion to write. Her "6-minute Stories" podcasts include: "Eye of the Dolphin," "Artist Borne," "Gobsmacked in the Gulfstream," "Renegade Daughter," "It Started with a Typo," "Shopping for the Homeless," "Thirteen Candles in the Dark," "The Promise of Romance," "At Five & Ninety-Five, Mother Was a Star," "In the Heart of Trauma," "The Jig Is Up," "Getting a Head Start," and "Rum Punch and Reefers."

Shooting Stars
by Anne M. Middleton

My senior year of high school in Greenville, North Carolina, I had a sensational, unexpected romance with Drew Cooper, the most popular, swoon-worthy boy in town. Later, years after going off to college and barely seeing one another, the old heartthrob and I were about to give it another shot.

Drew had hit the DNA jackpot in the physical attributes category. He was six-foot-something with teddy-bear brown eyes and a muscled Adonis-body. He turned all the girls into giddy puddles of goo. But not me. I was committed to taking myself way too seriously to be charmed by the likes of Drew Cooper.

I had no time for silly crushes. I had high-level duties to attend to. I was the person who had been called to be the leader of that high school. That's right: *called*. I had won the election for student body president by a landslide majority in a field of six candidates, a mandate I fancied was unprecedented in the worldwide annals of high school presidential races.

It is axiomatic that a female who has been mandated to assume the mantle of teen leadership should not muddy up their dignity by going to mush over some football star that every cheerleader in the county was mooning over.

And plus: I wasn't Drew Cooper's type. I was a Hilary, not a Melania. I got plenty of appreciation from the boys in the marching band, the chess team, the National Honor Society. Boys who liked my sharp mind and quick wit, who didn't mind one bit that I was a tad over-ample of thigh and booty, that my hair was short and curly instead of long and sleek. Boys who regarded it as a plus that I had never once shaken a pom-pom or performed a herkie-jump. I was not a football player's type of gal.

But Drew Cooper turned out to be a subversive. Drew began ignoring the fawning cheerleaders. Drew paid no attention to the dimpled homecoming candidates and the lithe gymnasts. Day after day, Drew waited after class by one girl's locker: mine. Drew walked me to class, carried my books. Drew's teddy-bear brown eyes beamed at me in adoration.

This level of attention from charismatic Greek-god-looking creature is admittedly hard to resist. But still,: I had student council meetings to run, morning announcements to blast over the staticky intercom. I had student assemblies to preside over, candy bar fund-raisers to ride herd on.

I fought the good fight, but even a mandated leader of my caliber must eventually capitulate to the level of "will-they-or-won't-they," star-crossed, against-type opposites-attract kind of teenage first-love energy that was generated by this situation. The stars had aligned, and they weren't taking no for an answer. Drew and I became "a thing." A glorious, improbable thing.

Then we graduated. The stars got all wonked-up. I went to the University of North Carolina and Drew accepted a full football scholarship all the way across the country at UCLA. We kept in touch, saw each other on holidays. After college, I went to work in New York City, and Drew was still in Los Angeles with another year of football eligibility.

Finally, after nearly a year of not seeing each other, it happened that we would both be visiting our families back home in North Carolina at the same time during the summer. Drew invited me to come water-skiing at his family's river house on the Pamlico River, about 30 miles outside of our hometown. I set off for our reunion, my heart a-flutter. This special thing between us was still there, I could feel it. Maybe the stars were aligning once again.

About five miles outside of town, another car turned sharply in front of me. I slammed on brakes to avoid hitting it. My car spun in a 180-degree bat-turn and flipped over onto its roof. I crawled out of the upside-down wreckage through the window. I felt shaken, but uninjured.

First responders insisted that EMS check me out, so I climbed into the ambulance, lay down on the gurney, and found myself looking directly into the teddy-bear brown eyes of a six-foot something guy from my high school.

No, I wasn't delusional. And it wasn't Drew Cooper. It was a sweet, shy goober named Trent who'd played trumpet in the marching band and who was now working as an EMT. Trent was overjoyed to see me, grateful I checked out fine except for a cut on my knee. He kept marveling at the unexpected, odd reunion.

Shooting Stars

I felt those things, too: grateful to be OK, happy to see Trent. But I also felt a mournful disappointment about the reunion I was missing, about a constellation I now sensed would never align the same way again. •

Copyright 2025, Anne M. Middleton

Anne M. Middleton lives in Raleigh, North Carolina, where for over two decades she was the State of North Carolina's lead appellate attorney in the areas of crimes against children and adult sexual offenses. Since retirement, Anne enjoys writing, performing improv, and exploring spiritual traditions of mysticism and higher consciousness. She is a shamanic practitioner and member of the Foundation for Shamanic Studies, a Shamanic Reiki Master, a certified yoga teacher (RYT-500), an avid lucid dreamer and dream yoga practitioner, and a member of the International Association for the Study of Dreams.

Feline Education
by Tanya E. E. E. Schmid

A kitten can't tell the difference between a piece of string and a poisonous snake. My gray and white furball is sitting on a sun-warmed rock and confusing an Aspis Viper with the old black shoelace that I pull across our kitchen floor for entertainment.

I have learned a lot about vipers since we moved to the farm a couple years ago. Part of the beauty of our remote location is the abundant wildlife. Including the slithering kind. Normally, I would need my camera in order to zoom in on the snake's eye, to see if it has a devilish slit instead of a harmless round pupil. To see if there are more than one row of scales beneath the hinged mouth. But I know this four-foot-long viper. I have passed her almost daily on my walk to the woodpile, her perch set back far enough from the path not to pose a threat. Not a significant threat to a human, at least. Her bite holds a deadly portion of venom for a mouse…or other small animal.

Kitten's claws are sharp. But Pete just taps the silky black coils with his left front paw pads. Trying to get the thick string to move. To play.

"Pete!" I call out, knowing snakes are deaf, and trying to break my kitten's intense focus. I'm still frozen about six feet away so as not to upset the momentary balance.

Vipers aren't easily disturbed. Especially when they are sunning on their favorite rock. They play it cool. They know their powers well. Bites usually result from a blind step while picking blackberries. Thus, the knee-high rubber boots we purchased first thing. Snakes wait silently in the leafy shadows of the briars for those mice who crave fruit and are naïve enough to tempt fate.

My voice is ignored. The rope has come to life, its rings shifting slowly like a kaleidoscope. My kitten's eyes dilate in exhilaration.

Does the viper know that this little dude will grow into her competition for mice? No worries there. The mouse population on our two hectares abounds, which is why we bought a cat. No, the viper's not out for a fight. But God help anyone who wakes her from her beauty sleep.

My kitten lifts a white powder puff paw and holds it over the unwinding coils.

"Pete, no!" I step closer, softly because vibrations would alert the viper.

The biggest problem is the thin lattice of blackberry briars that form a loose net between me and my pet. My brain calculates the necessary angle and the odds of me successfully sweeping through the thorns with my bare arm and slapping Pete to the ground without either of us getting bit.

The small paw hangs for a moment, quivering, then Pete taps the coils again and the head of the snake pops up like the hook of a clothes hanger. The triangle head looms large in comparison to my grapefruit-sized pet and the pores on the back of my neck tingle. We are miles away from the nearest vet. Not much they could do anyway.

"Honey?" My husband's voice calls from the house. I know he sees me poised like a statue on our gravel drive, but I don't dare look away from my baby. "What's taking you so long?" he asks.

The screen door slams shut and his boots crunch towards me.

Wide kitten eyes fix in a staring contest with two slits, then Pete recognizes the problem and pulls back an inch or two. He raises himself slowly to his feet and his fuzz stands on end as he arches his back and stands sideways on tiptoe.

No way I'll be fast enough.

Then I notice the vines growing under the viper's perch. A split second to guess how heavy the rock is, if I could get it to tip back. I leap forward, just behind the snake, and yank at a handful of the creepers, thorns piercing my fingers.

It's just enough to give the throne a shudder, and Pete jumps down through the bushes and bounds away as the head of the black whip darts at his shadow.

"Didn't you hear me?" My husband arrives next to me.

Feline Education

"That snake almost bit Pete!"

"What snake?" my husband asks as we stare at an empty rock.

I hold my scratched hand while he gathers the wood I'd dropped a lifetime ago. Over his bent back, I spot Pete down by the newly planted apple trees, stalking a robin in the grass. •

Copyright 2025, Tanya E. E. E. Schmid

Born and raised in Wisconsin, Tanya E. E. E. Schmid was a Doctor of Oriental Medicine until 2014 when she started a permaculture farm near Bern, Switzerland. Her work has appeared in *The Fourth River*, *Valparaiso Fiction Review*, *Ponder Review*, *ENO*, *Sky Island Journal*, *Flash Fiction Magazine*, and others. Tanya was a finalist in Ruminate's The Waking Flash Contest. She is the author of "Tanya's Collection of Zen Stories," and is currently writing a novel. www.tanyaswriting.com

My Father Figure
by Akira Odani

Uncle Taka invited me on a fishing adventure for my 7th birthday. He met me before dawn with bamboo poles and a tackle box. We traveled by train and bus to a pier in Tokyo Bay. After purchasing a bag of squirming sandworms, we hired a bandana-clad, tattooed captain to take us on a small wooden dinghy a few miles to the breakwater. The morning sun showered us as we perched on the edge of giant rocks at the far end of a vast, sparkling bay. Sea breezes washed the city grime off our faces.

After watching my uncle's demonstrations, I whipped my fishing pole for the first time to cast my line.

"Ouch! What the heck?" yelled Uncle Taka.

"Oops! I'm sorry!"

The silvery hook at the end of my line snagged his earlobe. He patiently removed the sharp metal from his bleeding ear. With a friendly smile, he joked, "Akira, you caught a big fish!"

After a glorious, fun-filled day, we returned home sun-kissed, exhausted, and triumphant, with dozens of gobies.

Uncle Taka, my mother's brother, was a dashing young man with a perpetual smile, a broad forehead, and slicked-back hair. I admired him as my mentor, outdoor guide, storyteller, and musician. His life hadn't been easy; he lost both parents during his adolescence and barely survived the bombings in downtown Tokyo in the spring of 1945. Through determination and hard work, he lifted himself from the ashes of a devastated city by working at construction sites.

As the first in our family to obtain a driver's license, he rented a sedan and took the whole family, driving us leisurely along the Pacific coast. The smooth glide with the windows down, moving through green pine groves, made me feel like a caged bird set free into the open sky.

Some nights, my younger brothers and I would huddle around him, pleading for his stories. He lowered his voice as if sharing some closely guarded secrets.

"The other night, I took a shortcut home in the dark, walking through the cemetery. Behind a tall tombstone, I heard a rustling, scraping noise. I peeked behind the grave marker. Suddenly, a drooling black cat with glaring gold eyes loomed large over me. *Aghaghagh!*" He rose abruptly. We screamed with delight and giggled, knowing we were safe.

On a summer day, he took us swimming in a deeper part of the Tama River, where the Mitake Mountain range meets the Kanto plain. He showed us how to float and move our limbs. At one point, he lifted me onto his shoulders and began to cross the river. His chest, and then his face, sank below the surface. I shrieked in delight, holding onto his submerged head.

For my 10th birthday, he gave me a camera. I still treasure one of the few remaining black-and-white photographs of him strumming his guitar. His favorite song was Nino Rota's "La Strada," a nostalgic tune—my first live music experience.

Uncle Taka's visits were like sunlight breaking through dark rain clouds. In contrast, my father, whom I rarely saw, remained sad and melancholic. He acted as though his children were a burden. His love for us was as tepid as a samurai learning to be civil.

As a teenager, I took my uncle's presence for granted. However, I learned that bad things can happen to good people. One afternoon, shortly after I turned 15, my somber-looking mother grabbed me when I returned home from school. "Uncle Taka ... was in an accident. We must rush to the hospital."

The steel bucket of a construction crane struck him, crushing his skull between the heavy metal and the earthen wall. The detail shattered my so-far, tenuously happy life into bits and pieces.

When we arrived at the hospital, his body had already been taken to a facility for the terminally injured, situated next to a Buddhist temple, the location of the funeral. The attending nurse informed us that he was breathing but remained unconscious—there was no chance of recovery. With swollen, red eyes, my mother stepped out of his room and suggested it was my turn.

I shuddered at the sight of his body lying in a metal-framed bed. Bloodstained gauze was wrapped around his head, and his eyes were tightly shut. "Oomph!" he moaned and breathed heavily. I couldn't tell if he recognized my presence as I hovered by his bedside. *How could he lose his vibrancy so suddenly? Who did this?* I felt powerless to help. I bowed in silence and said goodbye to my guardian. He passed away hours later.

My uncle's life was taken in an instant. However, he gave me precious memories, planting a healthy seed within me to embrace life with joy. •

Copyright 2025, Akira Odani

Akira Odani lives in the historic city of St. Augustine, Florida. He is a member of the Taste Life Twice Writers' Group and the Florida Writers Association. Born in Tokyo, he graduated from International Christian University and earned his Ph.D. in Chinese History from Brown University. Some of his work has appeared in the pages of FWA anthologies, *Kaidankai* (Japanese ghost stories), and several versions of the Personal Story Publishing Project. His passion for writing comes from his ambition to understand the mystery of life and the world.

Just a Doodle?
by Janice Luckey

Ever since she was a little girl, our daughter loved playing with dolls—Barbie dolls, Cabbage Patch kids, Madame Alexander dolls. The scenario was always the same—mama, daddy, and two little girls which she dressed and undressed all day long. As she grew up, this was still her dream—to be married and have two little girls. She never wavered from this traditional choice for her life even in the face of the feminist culture of the time.

After kissing her share of frogs, she finally found her prince and married. Soon after, as planned, she became pregnant at the age of 37. Though doctors labeled her pregnancy as an Advanced Maternal Age Pregnancy the idea that her baby could have birth defects did not discolor the picture-perfect tableau she held in her mind. Mom. Dad. Two little girls. Doctors recommended a test to determine the possibility. She declined. "If the test was positive, what would I do about it?" she reasoned. "Could I end a life I have desperately wanted all my life? Wouldn't that be saying I know more than God?"

Late in her pregnancy when her weight gain was not keeping pace as expected, she did submit to the test which returned a positive diagnosis for Down syndrome. Now it was real. Her dream, she felt, lay in tatters. Over the next few weeks, she vacillated between denial and depression. At her lowest point, our daughter sobbed, "Mom, I don't know if I can even give this baby my favorite name." After her raw emotions ran their course, to her credit our daughter rose to the occasion. She began educating herself about the realities of raising a child with Down syndrome.

Tipping the scales at four pounds and four ounces, our first granddaughter arrived still shimmering with heaven's leavings. We counted ten fingers and ten toes and three 21st chromosomes confirming the Down syndrome diagnosis. Our family thought we were prepared to accept the challenging reality and bear the hardship this child would bring. Little did we know, tiny Merritt would not break our hearts. She would crack them wide open and enrich our lives beyond measure.

It is difficult to talk about kids with Down syndrome without using cliches and generalities. At the age of 10, yes, Merritt is jolly, but she can be grouchy when her sister gets on her last nerve. Yes, she is innocent, but she can be shrewd when sneaking a second helping of ice cream out of the freezer. Where she wins the prize is her capacity to love. Her love is all inclusive. Merritt shows an extra helping of compassion, too, especially if someone near her is sick. She dons her play stethoscope, thermometer, and brings her blood pressure cuff along with Band-Aids and bandages to treat her patient. We thought raising her would be a difficult joy, but most of the time it is plain joy.

A scene from the movie *Peanut Butter Falcon* illustrates the character of a person with Down syndrome. In this movie,

Zak, a young adult with Down syndrome, is about to fulfill his dream of wrestling his hero. Zak's coach tries to teach him to talk smack to his opponent. "Say mean things to him," the coach advises. "Talk about his mama! Just say the vilest thing you can think of." Zak catches on fast and jumps into the ring bursting forth with his most evil jab—"You can't come to my birthday party!"

Can you imagine a world where one's worst thought is *you can't come to my birthday party*? That is an example of our world with Merritt in it. Like Zak in the movie, she loves nothing better than a good birthday party and wants everyone to come. She often confuses which family member is celebrating a birthday, but every goodbye holds a reminder, "See you at my birthday party." Simple all-inclusive love.

Our daughter is indeed living her lifelong dream of mothering two little girls. Would she do it all again? Her answer? An unequivocal *yes!* The dream is still intact as she watches both girls dressed in superhero costumes playing Barbies on the living room rug.

A sketch by my artist mother-in-law of a little girl with a wide brimmed bonnet hangs in our home. She called the drawing just a "doodle" that she was going to throw away before I snapped it up for my own. This beloved piece of art reminds me of all the children with special needs, how they are like that doodle some would disregard and toss aside. On the contrary, we should treasure them as wonderful masterpieces created in the image of God. •

Copyright 2025, Janice Luckey

Janice Luckey, who lives in Mooresville, North Carolina, remembers when writing became a rhythm of her life. She scribbled a romance novel in a 3-ring binder in junior high school sparking a life-long love of all things writerly—writing, reading, journaling and hoarding office supplies. Janice is fueled by the love and support of her family and most anything chocolate. When not writing, she can be found making memories with her husband and four granddaughters, or roaming the aisles at the library, bookstores, and Staples.

Just Desserts
by Robin Russell Gaiser

In Room 206 on Jefferson 2nd Floor East, blue-lidded Tupperware containers of dark, moist brownies and large chocolate chip cookies nestled on the top shelf of my roommate Eleanor's closet. We were freshmen at The College of William and Mary. The homemade treats, baked by her mother, showed up at least twice a month. Eleanor's older brother Larry willingly transported their mother and the goodies six hours round trip from Alexandria to Williamsburg, Virginia, and back again in his muscled, polished black Dodge Charger. The delectables remained Eleanor's sole property.

Eleanor began noticing that her sweet stash was diminishing and called her mother, a wry older woman, four times married, with thick glasses, big hands and grandmotherly attire. "I'll take care of this, honey."

Once we knew things were in those large hands, Eleanor and I mused about just who had the gall to enter our room and steal her food.

"You think Jodie or Pat would do it? They're right next door," I said. "Easy to slip in and out."

"Unlikely. Both pre-med. They study all the time. And they're too short to reach the shelf," said Eleanor.

"How about Ruthie or Jane? I've noticed Ruthie's gained some weight," Eleanor said.

"Nope. They both keep Kosher."

"How do you know *that*?" she asked, then shook her head. "Of course, you know because you know *everybody*!" She was right. I made friends easily. She did not.

Our own circle from Jefferson 2nd East, Linda and Paula, Betsy, Gerry, Ellen, and Jo knew the rules about the Tupperware goodies. But when all of us gathered in someone's room after dinner before our studies commenced, the desserts were offered freely. I wondered if Eleanor thought this was the way to make friends.

I considered mentioning Celia Ann as a possible thief but dismissed the idea. Celia Ann Blevins had the only single room on our hall. She was beautiful, rich, a spoiled only child schooled at a tony private school in Richmond. Her closet overflowed with the best and latest styles. Her mother brought the family's maid along once a month to re-stock Celia Ann with snacks, clothing, and toiletries and to clean and straighten Celia Ann's dirty, disheveled room. The rest of us cleaned our own rooms. Asking Celia Ann to share her bounty was pointless. What was hers was hers. She didn't need a thing.

The sweets continued to disappear. Five days after Eleanor's revelations of loss, Larry and their mother arrived bearing loaded Tupperware containers and two bulging shoe boxes, rustling with wax paper as Larry set them down on Eleanor's desk.

With sparkling eyes magnified through her lenses, and a smirk on her face, Eleanor's mother instructed us not to eat the Tupperware fare but to store it in its usual place on the top shelf. And to stow the shoe boxes elsewhere and enjoy those goodies.

After she and Larry left to drive home, and after we enjoyed a fresh brownie or two, we wrapped the shoe boxes in a small blanket and placed them in my suitcase, already on its side, closed the lid and slid it under my bed.

The thief must have smelled the freshly baked brownies and cookies when she opened our door the next morning. And she must have imbibed in several helpings, since that afternoon we heard heavy footsteps racing down the hallway to the gang bathroom at the end of the corridor. These episodes, accompanied by vociferous groaning and sharp expletives, continued into the evening.

Eleanor and I dragged our stocky dark wooden desk chairs up to our door to peer over the open transom at the long hall. There was beautiful, entitled Celia Ann Blevins doubled over in gastric distress *en route* to the john. We doubled over in hysterics.

Later that evening we joined our concerned hall mates, who also had heard the commotion, as Celia Ann explained that her affliction must have come from something she ate in the college cafeteria (actually a believable tale).

We knew the source of all the drama. *Ex Lax* pastries had delivered the "just desserts."

When we eventually shared the truth about Celia Ann's misery with each of our hall mates, several of them reported food and snacks missing from their rooms. Eleanor's mother's clever solution to the thieving had them doubled over in hysterics, too.

After that, Jefferson 2nd Floor East locked its doors. And Eleanor's chocolate delights remained safe in their Tupperware bins stowed on her top closet shelf in Room 206.

I must admit at that point in our lives, we had not learned that someone who appears to have everything, can still feel terribly empty. •

Copyright 2025, Robin Russell Gaiser

Robin majored in English at The College of William and Mary. In "those days," creative writing was absent from the heady curriculum, although Robin wrote poetry which was published in several lit magazines. After college, she taught high school English in Fairfax, Virginia. Creative writing was included in Robin's classrooms. Robin has written two memoirs, both published by Pisgah Press, multiple short stories and essays, and, of course, poetry. A third book, a collection of all genres of Robin's writing, is nearing completion. Robin and her husband live in Asheville, North Carolina. www.robingaiser.com

Strike Up the Band
by Joel R. Stegall

What passed in the US Army for the Camp Leroy Johnson band in New Orleans during the fall of 1963 bore only a vague resemblance to an actual instrumental ensemble. The group was made up of whatever enlisted men played, or claimed to play, an instrument. Volunteers were not hard to come by because if you were in the band, you could sometimes avoid unpleasant duties such as KP—"kitchen patrol."

The band had to have an officer to provide a connection with the chain of command. When the personnel people saw this lieutenant had a music degree, I was assigned as band officer. Never mind that I knew nothing about bands—my expertise and interest was choral music. Fortunately, the CLJ band director, Pfc. Benson, was an intelligent and decent person and I could count on him to do what was needed at the right time. As it happened, his father was a US congressman from Wisconsin.

This rag-tag instrumental ensemble played only for ceremonial occasions, such as when the post commandant wanted a parade for another congressman, a New Orleans native and member of the US House Armed Services Committee. An order came down to me to have the band looking sharp, sounding good, and ready to lead the parade. In *The Music Man*, Harold Hill described the magic of 76 trombones leading a big parade. Our band had maybe fifteen players total, and only one trombone.

At the time of the congressman's parade, several players, including the sole trombonist, were in the post stockade. I reported to my superiors that if the commandant wanted a band, he might want to find a way to temporarily release the trombone player and his buddies for this patriotic assignment. The cause may not have been at the level of the heroics of those in the movie, *The Dirty Dozen*, but it was nonetheless deemed worthy.

When this small ensemble marched past the reviewing stand, the sound was raunchy, but the fatigue uniforms were cleaned and pressed and the players marched more-or-less together. And we had our trombone player. It wasn't quite as glorious as Harold Hill's description of what a band could be in River City, but avoiding a catastrophe in The Big Easy was good enough.

In May 1961, President Kennedy had challenged the country to put a man on the moon before the end of the decade. A critical part of this ambitious plan was the National Aeronautics and Space Administration's Apollo space program. The launch vehicle that would hurl a capsule through the Earth's gravitational pull and into space was the five-stage Saturn Five rocket. When I was at Camp Leroy Johnson, Saturn Five's first stage, the booster, was being built at NASA's Michoud Assembly Facility in New Orleans. When it was completed in the fall of 1963, it would be shipped by barge over the Intracoastal Waterway to Cape Canaveral, Florida, where it would be assembled with other components and launched into space.

To celebrate the completion of the booster, a ceremony was planned for early December at the Michoud plant. Vice President Lyndon Johnson, charged with oversight of the space program, was to be the keynote speaker. As Camp Leroy Johnson was the closest military base, the CLJ band was invited to perform. My job was to coordinate the band's part of the ceremony which I would attend. On a visit to the Michoud facility to work out details, I walked past this monumental testament to American engineering. Its size was overwhelming: 163 feet high, tall as a sixteen-story building, and thirty-three feet in diameter.

That December I was going to be present and my band performing at a public celebration of one of the most ambitious phases of the nation's effort to put a man on the moon, and I would be in the same room with the Vice President of the United States.

Everything was set. Then Marshall Bowens, a young Black enlisted man in my platoon, was charged by New Orleans police with resisting arrest.

Uh-oh. •

(Continued in "The Truth Comes Out")

Strike Up the Band

Copyright 2025, Joel R. Stegall

In his career as professor and academic administrator, Joel Stegall wrote more than 35 journal articles, book chapters, opinion pieces and other such. None of these gained him widespread acclaim. Since retiring to Winston-Salem, North Carolina, he has written a family history tracing his ancestry back to 1735. Though documentation is elusive, he has found considerable evidence that his ancestry began even earlier. Several of his stories, often about his ancestors, have appeared in the Personal Stories Publishing Project. Joel continues to write because he likes to.

The Truth Comes Out
by Joel R. Stegall

While planning for the Saturn Five booster ceremony in December 1963, as a lieutenant and officer in charge of the band, I still had to deal with day-to-day issues at Camp Leroy Johnson. When Marshall Bowens, a young Black enlisted man in my platoon, was charged by New Orleans police with resisting arrest, I got involved as much as I could. [This story continues from "Strike Up the Band."]

Bowens's story was that after being stopped in a routine traffic check, the white policeman told Bowens to move on. To Bowens's surprise, as he drove off, the cop yelled at him. When Bowens stopped to see what the problem was, the officer said he had told Bowens to pull over to the shoulder. Bowens explained that he had misunderstood the instructions, but that didn't matter; the officer charged him with resisting arrest. Bowens could pay a fine or go to court. Facing a relatively small fine and no jail time, some would have paid the fine and moved on. But Bowens felt he couldn't do that because he was not guilty. He would explain his case to a judge.

Bowens was scheduled to appear in New Orleans Traffic Court at 11:00 am, Friday, November 22. I rode to the courthouse on Rampart Street with Bowens in his old Mercury.

With no legal representation, Bowens told the judge his side of the story. Following protocol, I stood beside Bowens before the judge but was not permitted to say anything. (I could have testified that I knew Bowens to be fine young man.) Bowens ended with something like: *I respected the officer and assumed he would also respect me.* When he said that, the policeman, sitting only a few feet behind us, said, "I guess you found out about that …." I was stunned with the obvious contempt he held for this young African American who was serving his country. The judge, who did not hear this or, more likely, ignored it, contemplated only a few seconds and then announced that Bowens should pay the fine. Bowens did, and we were out of the courtroom before noon.

Arriving back at Bowens's car, we found one tire was flat. As Bowens changed the tire, a man walked by and told us the governor of Texas had been shot. I didn't make much of it; we were only three blocks from Bourbon Street where it was not all that unusual to hear strange people say strange things, even during daylight hours. However, we were curious, and as soon as we got in the car, we turned on the radio and learned that both Texas Governor John Connelly and President Kennedy had been shot while riding in a Dallas parade. Their conditions were not known.

Back at Camp Leroy Johnson, I walked into the company orderly room to an eerie quiet. Nobody even pretended to work as everyone hovered around a small black-and-white TV. At 1:38 p.m., we heard Walter Cronkite announce, "From Dallas, Texas…, President Kennedy died at 1 p.m. Central Standard Time, 2 o'clock Eastern Standard Time, some 38 minutes ago."

It seemed incomprehensible that the President of the United States, the most powerful man in the world with, we thought, the best security possible, could be gunned down in an American city in the presence of thousands of people. To me, and to many in my generation, Kennedy symbolized the hope for renewed vigor in our country based on ideas, imagination, and determination. This was not just the assassination of the President; it was the death of hopes and dreams. And it called into question fundamental questions about national security. *Who did it? Why? Was the nation itself at risk—from outsiders or from our own?*

While most Americans mourned Kennedy's death, I was shocked to find that some were delighted. Was race involved with those reactions? Were we seeing the same contempt I had witnessed by that police officer in court? After all, the President had come to Texas as a favor to his vice-president, to help smooth over racially charged tensions after Kennedy sent 20,000 US Army soldiers to quell the riots in Oxford, Mississippi, and to ensure the integration of Ole' Miss despite the deeply contested enrollment of James Meredith, a Black man. On Sunday morning two days later, when I picked up my toddler son from our church nursery, one of the workers said she was glad somebody finally got Kennedy. The pastor at a Dallas church preached about letting go of hate. His life was threatened, sending him and his family into hiding in fear for their lives.

With the assassination of President Kennedy, the Saturn Five booster celebration was cancelled; Lyndon Johnson had more important things to do. The nation muddled through more years of contentious racial animus, but the space program continued with renewed energy, and four years later, on November 9, 1967, the Saturn Five rocket, with the booster I had seen in New Orleans' Michoud plant, thrust America one step closer to putting a man on the moon. •

Copyright 2025, Joel R. Stegall

Since retiring to Winston-Salem, North Carolina, Joel Stegall has completed a family history dating from the early Colonial Era. Longer (and more interesting) than any scholarly work he ever wrote, he was pleased to find in his bloodline literary ability, ingenuity, inventiveness, devotion to duty, self-sacrifice and uncommon love. At the same time, he was taken aback to discover insanity, murder, suicide and cattle rustling.

Stuck in the Second Stage
by Kym B. Whitecar

It happened to me again this morning, innocently watching CBS's *Sunday Morning*. A feature about the actress June Squibb aired. The show reported that she became an overnight sensation for her role in "Nebraska" in 2013. Her performance earned her an Academy Award nomination at the age of 84. Currently, she is debuting as the lead in the action-comedy "Thelma." Do you know what my mother did at that age? She died!

Whenever I learn about another senior celebrating their 100th birthday, starting a new career in their 80s, or living until the age of 110, it infuriates me. These overachievers get under my skin. Admittedly, the real source of my irritation is my mother's early exit. Any excuse she could give wouldn't cut it. Her mother lived until 92, and her grandmother was five months shy of 100. Genetics didn't factor into her rash demise.

My warped resentment started ten years earlier after Dad died. His failing health generated several scares that prepared us for the reality of the situation. After he passed, I found myself having angry discussions with my father once similar stories came to my attention. I held them up as proof of his premature desertion. Weirdly, this one-sided chat would comfort me. He mostly just listened to me rage on as a hormonal (but justified) teen. Feeling understood helped then and now, cushioning the fact that he had held on for as long as he could.

Unlike her spouse, Mother didn't act like someone signaling for the departure lane. Every day she walked on her treadmill and ate a well-balanced diet (except for the gallons of Mountain Dew she drank). She drove to the farmer's market to pick up in-season produce and to the library for her favorite author's latest novel. We couldn't hide much from her. Once she got something in her head the jaws of life couldn't extract it. Unexpectedly, she started talking about welcoming death. As these rants ramped up, we didn't take them seriously, thinking her pedigree would be her undoing.

Eventually, it became apparent that living by herself was no longer possible. We struggled with placement. Ultimately a sister told Mom she would be packed up and moved into her home. Those of us with some form of counseling degree burned through each technique we had as Mom fussed long distance. A sibling licensed in real estate made arrangements to get her house on the market. Our Air Force major used military precision to organize, box, and transport. The youngest wisely stayed out of the fray. Astonishingly Mom's relocation happened.

We had many reasons to justify Mom living with us but assumed longevity and outlasting her retirement accounts were the main ones. She had a different motivation, only agreeing to this arrangement to avoid whittling away our inheritance on her subsistence. Mom's maxim: *If I told you once I told you a thousand times* looped in my head as she repeated, "That money is for you kids."

As Mother made the rounds from one child's house to another, each was resoundingly rejected. Texas and Florida had the double whammy of heat and humidity. Utah's frosty winters were intolerable. She couldn't deal with the "menagerie" of pets (two dogs and one cat in different locations) with the nerve to sit beside her or look in her room. She slammed doors left open to air out rooms and hid night lights that dared illuminate her way. Despite her efforts, we did not comply with her demands.

The proverbial push shoved us into a new course of action. She chose an assisted living apartment and settled in more relieved than happy. However, just as she had discarded each of our homes, issues developed with her retirement community. The activities director constantly interrupted her Bingo boycott by inviting her to participate. Staff wanted her to wear an alert button which she promptly lost. The menu's deficiencies required supplementary trips to Sprouts to find raspberries, chocolate muffins, or divinity. Small concessions did occur. I played it cool when my mother proudly displayed a pink manicure. As her abilities decreased, her discontent grew. She tried to spread her frustration, but her nurse aides just smiled and called her "spicy." Switching tactics, she announced that she wanted to return to Tucson, not to live but to—*surprise!*—die. Again, we did not hear her. We endured eye rolls and dagger-filled glares as we saw no other option.

Mom's vindication arrived. Approximately 10 years before her mother and 20 years before her grandmother she checked out permanently. Looking at her in her casket, I swear I could see the hint of a smile. *I told you so* rang in my ears. She had won with her estate pretty much intact doing what she had wanted.

Stuck in the Second Stage

I guess that is what 94-year-old June Squibb is doing now despite my annoyance and grief. •

Copyright 2025, Kym B. Whitecar

Kym B. Whitecar lives in Indian Trail, North Carolina, where she is a member of the Charlotte Writers Club and Charlotte Lit. When she retired from education, she finally had the time to take a creative writing course, reigniting her passion for storytelling. This is her first published work. Currently, she is harassing her friends, family, and critic group with more narrative nonfiction.

The Perfect Imperfect
by Alison Rice Bruster

It was going to be the trip of a lifetime. Now that we were retired, we could travel without the constraint of a one or two-week break from work. Instead, we would have a month to make our way at our leisure from one end of Italy to the other. My husband, Terry, and I had each been there earlier in our lives, but we had never experienced it together. We spent months researching and planning to craft an itinerary full of new places to explore, old favorites to revisit, and experiences to savor. That was the plan, anyway.

We landed in Milan and spent our first afternoon walking around atop the roof of the Duomo, seeing that iconic, gothic cathedral from a new perspective and feeling like we were off to a great start. The next day, we picked up our rental car and drove to Varenna, a village on the shore of Lake Como. As we wandered through a botanical garden overlooking the placid lake, I felt my heart rate slow as we fell into the languid pace of the place. So far, so good.

But my heart rate picked up a bit when we drove the Sella Pass, a 10-mile stretch through the towering Dolomite Mountains, a nerve-wracking experience on a narrow road with seemingly endless 180-degree switchbacks. It was like a rollercoaster ride without brakes, but with altitude. We were feeling pretty good about our ability to navigate the treacherous territory. Then we saw cyclists climbing the same extreme path under their own power and realized what weenies we were—but as travelers on vacation, we felt absolved.

When we reached Venice, it was—as it often is—drowning in a sea of cruise ship passengers and other day-trippers. However, we followed advice we had been given and "walked toward the tail of the fish" to escape the crowds and see the part of Venice where people actually live. We rambled through a quiet neighborhood of houses adorned with clotheslines full of laundry, spent time in a beautiful park on the waterfront, and discovered a stadium with a soccer match underway and a riotous crowd cheering their team on. It was a glorious afternoon.

The trouble started with a tickle in the back of Terry's throat in Vernazza, on the coast in the Cinque Terra. He mentioned that he must be allergic to something in the environment there, but neither of us thought much about it.

By the time we got to Florence and hauled our bags up three winding flights of stairs to our room, Terry was miserable. It was October 2022, and the world was emerging from the COVID pandemic, so I ventured out to a pharmacy for cough drops and COVID tests. He tested positive; I was negative. We did what we could to soothe his symptoms, canceled our plans, and mostly stayed in our room.

We had no choice but to keep moving south, since we had to end up in Rome for our flight home at the end of the trip. By the time we got to Sienna, I tested positive too, and we were both so sick that we stayed in our room and slept the entire time, emerging only to find something to eat.

At this point we were despondent, feeling like we were sleeping our way across Italy.

When we reached Orvieto, a hill town in Umbria, we collapsed into bed and took long naps. When we awoke, even though we just wanted to go back to sleep, we made ourselves take a walk. A quaint sandwich shop/wine bar we passed caught our eye, so we got a Porchetta sandwich to share and a couple glasses of wine.

We sat on a bench in the alleyway across from the shop and had an impromptu picnic. Porchetta is an Italian specialty that was new to us. It is a pork shoulder, stuffed with herbs, wrapped in the pork skin, roasted and sliced. The moist, savory, salty flavor of the sandwich exploded in my mouth, and the wine complimented it perfectly. As we ate, we watched people walking by and marveled at the way the late afternoon sunlight illuminated the cobblestone streets, brick archways, and irregular stone walls of the buildings.

In that moment, we stopped feeling sorry for ourselves and remembered why we came. Despite all the preparations we had made and the exciting activities we had lined up along the way, this quiet moment remains our favorite memory from the trip.

And I still think about how that perfect moment in a perfect place under imperfect circumstances might not have happened if things had gone according to plan. •

The Perfect Imperfect

Copyright 2025, Alison Rice Bruster

After a career spent finding the voices of senior business executives, Alison Rice Bruster is writing a new chapter. She holds a BA in English Literature from Queens University of Charlotte. This is her third story included in a collection from the Personal Story Publishing Project. She is a member of the Charlotte Writers Club, Charlotte Lit, and the North Carolina Writers Network. When they are not out traveling in search of adventure, Alison and her husband Terry live in Fort Mill, South Carolina.

A Christmas Surprise
by Annette L. Brown

Until I was 32, the same year my grandfather died and my son Matt was born, Santa visited my grandparents' house every Christmas Eve. Bright-eyed baby cousins, graying aunties, and everyone in between sat on Santa's lap. Family members requested elaborate gifts—Lamborghinis, rare jewels, trips to the Bahamas—but inevitably ended with, "What I really want, Santa, is a flashlight." Then Santa-Uncle or Santa-Cousin, whoever donned the velvet suit sewn by my grandmother's hand, would "Ho-Ho-Ho" and pull a flashlight from his hefty sack. I never knew why a flashlight, but I loved it.

I missed that tradition, which was lost with my grandparents' passing, and I cherished those memories. By the time Matt was 3, that loss spurred me into action. I would manufacture a "Santa Sighting" to create a memory for Matt. I would buy the requisite suit in town. My husband Joe would play Santa. I would sneak Matt into position to see Santa. *Voila!* We would delight in hearing Matt's morning-after story. *What could go wrong?*

"Sweetheart, wake up. Santa's here." I wiggled sleepy-boy's hand a bit. When he didn't budge, I nudged his shoulder. And then again with urgency. "Wake up! But Shhhh. Santa can't see us." *Or hear us.*

Matt peeked at me with one eye, then rolled over. "Oh, no you don't." I began pulling him by his arms into a sitting position. "We're." *When did he get so heavy?* "Gonna." *Sleeping kids don't have bones.* "See." *It's like lifting jelly!* "Santa!" *Heavy jelly.* Matt sat, teetering a bit, blinking slowly. I lifted him from bed, gripped him under the armpits, and directed his steps as he padded down the hallway. "Shhh," I repeated when we settled against the doorframe and leaned around the corner.

Santa-Joe stood from his crouched position, one foot in the cold firebox and one on the hearth, so it looked like he had just slid down the chimney. As he emerged from the fireplace, he chuckled, "Ho-Ho-Ho," then got to work stuffing the stockings and placing gifts under the tree, nibbling the cookies and gulping the milk. I couldn't see Matt's eyes because I stood behind him, but I imagined them as round as quarters! Staying quiet must have challenged him.

"Look, Santa likes the cookies we made him," I pointed out.

"Ummm" Matt purred.

"Come on, Sweetheart. We'll sneak you back to bed," I whispered when Santa-Joe turned back toward the fireplace. Settling Matt beneath the covers and kissing his forehead, I congratulated myself on a plan well executed!

Matt awakened before a hint of daylight, then boomeranged back from the living room entrance to our bedroom door, squealing, "Wake up, wake up! Santa came!" Our anticipation of hearing Matt tell us about seeing Santa pushed us from the warm blankets to the couch: Joe pulling a hoodie over his head, me looping a scrunchy around my ponytail, both of us wishing for a steaming cup of coffee. But first, Matt's story!

Matt stretched for his stocking on tippy-toes. Using both hands to slide it from its mantel hook, he cradled it and settled on the floor. Thinking I'd help him get started, I asked Matt, "Sweetheart, did you see Santa last night?"

He said nothing. Instead, Matt shot his arm into the air to display a container of bubbles fetched from the stocking.

I studied him, hunched over his prize, brown eyes intent on his ferreting. I leaned forward a bit and tried again. "Did you like seeing Santa?"

He glanced our way, brows furrowed and lips pursed, "Weeell." Then he grabbed a T-rex, "Look!" and returned to digging for deeper treasures.

Joe and I exchanged shrugs and raised eyebrows.

"Hey, a tractor book! And a kale-scope!" Matt yanked the kaleidoscope from the stocking, raised it to his eye and turned it. "Wwooooowww."

"Aren't you excited you got to see Santa?" Joe prodded.

Matt shook his head in a decisive "No" as he turned the stocking upside down to shower the carpet with a Pez

A Christmas Surprise

dispenser, rubber ball, and other tiny treasures that had been lodged in the toe.

"You didn't like seeing Santa?" I pressed.

"Mooom!" he retorted on an exaggerated exhale. "My body was up. But my eyes were down!"

"Your eyes were–" I began.

"Down?" Joe finished.

"What?!" Joe and I blurted together, our jaws hanging open. We both began slow nods, which evolved to grins, grew to resigned chuckles and swelled to full-belly laughter, the kind that makes your sides ache. We certainly had created a memory—just not the one we expected!

That Christmas I learned that regardless of careful plans gone completely wrong, any experience that ends in laughter, warms and brightens our lives.

Just like a flashlight. •

Copyright 2025, Annette L. Brown

Annette L. Brown is a mother, wife, and retired teacher, who lives on an almond farm in Central California where she enjoys spending time with family and friends. She is grateful for the support of The Taste Life Twice Writers and The Light Makers' Society and for simply having time to write. Annette has pieces reflecting her love of nature, family, beauty, and humor in several publications including *Pictura Journal*, *Last Stanza Poetry*, *Flash Fiction Magazine*, *Every Day Fiction*, and other PSP Project anthologies.

Choices About Love
by Ginny Foard

My parents, Will and Kat, did not intend to start their married life with extra mouths to feed. Their letters say so. Of course, later they told their kids that they loved us all. Usually they added, "despite the headaches you caused us."

Money was tight. Before their wedding, my father started his first professional job as an engineer in Baltimore, Maryland. Meanwhile, as engaged women did in 1949, my mom quit her job as a research physicist at the National Bureau of Standards. She managed wedding planning from her parents' home in Gaffney, South Carolina.

My father wrote to his fiancée, "having to tighten our belts—for meals I chew my fingernails or an ol' sock (could you slip me a fin?)." Days before their wedding, my dad wrote "with luck, I'll arrive in Gaffney with about 2 bucks… [and] a beautiful new suit." He described their new home to her, "Am using the small suitcase as a chair & have the lamp made out of two cans and an extension cord."

My parents hoped to enjoy a few years of marriage before children appeared. My mom summed up a story about a friend's child with, "I guess I've got a long way to go in learning to be tolerant with children." Their letters talk about contraceptives. Two weeks before the wedding, my mom told my dad to "be prepared, darlin', unless you think we'll be rich enough to feed three mouths nine months from now!"

Child One arrived nine months, five days after the wedding. Late in his life, my dad told me, "I know when that happened. It was on the train ride from Gaffney to Baltimore."

A few short years later, my mom inadvertently got my dad a pay raise. They'd invited his boss and his wife over for dinner. While chatting with them about children and my mom's news of (yet) another pregnancy, my mom remarked, "I don't know how we're going to feed them all." She was just being a gracious Southern hostess sharing common ground with her guests about life's mysteries. She didn't give it another thought until my dad came home from work with news that he'd just gotten a raise.

My parents' budget stayed tight. They kept close track of the good mileage by Petunia, the light-blue Volkswagen "bug" that carried the complete family. My dad decided to add space to their small house. With a spoon borrowed from the kitchen silverware, he began digging a hole in the dirt under the house's foundation. Months and long hours of sweat and tired muscles later, it was the doorway into a new basement.

When my mom was pregnant with their fourth child and the house bulged with three, high-energy, independent-minded adventurers under five years old, my dad's co-workers had thoughts. "You've got to do something about this," they jibed him.

My parents decided to stop the unabated stream of babies. My dad went to get a vasectomy. The doctor consulted with him for some time. The doctor saw a handsome man in his 30s. Probably he grasped my dad's lighthearted enjoyment of life, including its problems. He knew of my dad's responsibilities to his wife and four small children.

He probably did not know about my dad's fun pulling neighborhood kids' snow sleds behind Petunia. Or my dad's love of jitterbugging with my mom, or that when a man from Arthur Murray's studio saw my dad dancing before he shipped overseas in World War II, he invited my dad to teach dance in New York when he was back from the war.

Whatever the doctor saw that day, he had a clear opinion. He obviously did not know my dad's character. My dad, who had slapped a prostitute in wartime London when she propositioned him, then reported himself to a nearby bobby to avoid getting in trouble with the police. "If you get this operation," the doctor counseled, "you won't have a reason to stay faithful to your wife. You have a family that depends on you. Don't do this surgery."

My dad listened. He respected professional advice. He consulted with my mom. He did not schedule the surgery. He loved his family and wanted to keep it that way.

I know this story well. All my life, I listened as my dad—and sometimes my mom too—would recount this big decision moment. Then my dad would reach over to grab my hand or to hug me, saying, "I'm so glad that doctor talked us out of it."

Choices About Love

Soon after the doctor's consult, I was on the way—the fifth child.

Late in my parents' lives, I overheard my dad tell my mom, "I wish I could take Ginny and introduce her to that doctor, to show him the result of his advice." •

Copyright 2025, Ginny Foard

Ginny's parents had storytelling in their bones. Will's hands reenacted stories, swooping up high or spinning across the table with an ice cream spoon while he added sound effects from an array of odd noises he'd been fine-tuning since his childhood. Kat read aloud from a thick storybook of Irish or English classics, with appropriate accents and engaging expressions. Except! She would often ask Ginny to pick out a book and then read it to her, while Kat stood ironing clothes from the large laundry basket. Ginny loved it all. She lives in a little post office box on Sullivan's Island, South Carolina.

Going for the Gold
by Thomas Gery

At the age of 40, my work life in a child welfare agency was thriving. The Director of Development position came with excellent pay and benefits and significant professional autonomy. The organization had virtually no history. My role was to develop community recognition, obtain grants to begin new services, and establish an annual giving program. On the home front, life was in order: a devoted spouse; two healthy children; a farmhouse home; many friends; finances sound with two incomes. Life was good.

Then a new decade brought a sense of restlessness to my work life, or perhaps a letdown, following two major accomplishments. I had written successful proposals for a special-needs adoption service and a serious-juvenile-offenders treatment program. Each received substantial start-up grants Parentless, throw-away children and teens with mental, emotional, or serious medical problems were united with caring parents through adoption. Juvenile offenders, serious law breakers, received an opportunity to change. I was doing worthwhile work and doing it well

The type of agency-development work I did was not in a league with professional fund raising firms. I felt good when an annual, year-end mailing netted us 10 or 15 thousand dollars. With my team, I prepared a thoughtful letter describing a need, added some graphics or artwork reinforcing the message, combined it with a self-addressed stamped envelope, and waited. Easy. No stress.

After I observed a professional fundraiser make a sales presentation, the mind whispered, "I can do that." Over the next two years I would join and then depart, that same firm. The boredom I thought I was leaving was, in reality, a safe harbor. And the "I-can-do-that" opportunity I jumped into turned out to be uncharted, roiling waters with tempestuous seas. Psychologically, it was a dark time.

With my loving wife's blessing, I took on several life events simultaneously, any one of which would be highly stressful. Within the span of three months, I changed jobs (causing a cut in overall remuneration), added debt with the purchase of a home in the city, relocated the family there and became a landlord by turning the family farmhouse into a rental property.

A significant part of my new role as a fundraising consultant was invested in capital campaigns conducted by nonprofit charitable organizations. It's a huge undertaking involving major financial gifts from individuals who are honored by receiving naming rights. One has to be comfortable in the upper levels of society where wealth and status are concentrated. I was not but did not know it.

My memory and diary inform this story. Between June 1990 and October 1992, the words "stress," "pressure," "anxiety" appear on page after page. So do thoughts relating to success, although not often enough to assuage fear. And references to a spiritual renewal are scrawled on the paper. On June 28, 1992, my wife and I attended Billy Graham's Philadelphia Crusade. The next day's entry captured a feeling: "It was inspiring. All I have to do is believe in Jesus and everything will be ok." These pages scream desperation and a search for relief.

My family was there for me. My spouse approved of the risk taking and showed it with her emotional support. She took on extra hours as a nurse to buttress the finances. The kids—little, innocent and appropriately oblivious—provided inspiration and motivation.

I became overwhelmed by moving one level too high in the fund-raising profession. In the business world, it's called the "Peter Principle"—moving one level beyond your competency. The two-year experiment ended. The brass-ring grab for increased wealth and status resulted in the diminishment of both. My next job brought a fifty percent pay cut, little professional autonomy, and weekend hours. But the supervisory position in a children's mental health program had what I needed. I was in well-charted waters with calm seas; the heavy dark storm cloud of anxiety became clear, blue sky.

My sunset years illuminate the past. I remember my dad often saying to me, the young child, "You are a good boy but a poor boy." When my own inner voice whispered "You can do this" I believe it was a hard *no* to my father's words. Culturally we abhor failure, yet learning from mistakes makes us stronger. I failed to gain the gold, but the "good boy" weathered the storm. From my vantage point in my eighth decade, I see the long-ago experience defined by the adage, "All is well that ends well." •

Copyright 2025, Thomas Gery

Thomas Gery, a common man with uncommon experiences lives in Berks County, Pennsylvania. He served in the U.S. Army with duty in Vietnam. As a social worker he helped children, youth, and adults in a variety of practice venues and situations throughout a work life of 40 years. Married with two adult children and two grandchildren, he is currently writing his life's story to provide answers to questions his kids will never ask. His earliest published stories have appeared in Personal Story Publishing Project—*Lost & Found*, *Sooner or Later*, *Now or Never*, and *Foolhardy*.

Operation New TV
by Lisa Williams Kline

The time I had dreaded had come. The strange black dot on our TV screen, which made it look like golfers had an alternate hole to aim for, or that people in close-up had a large mole, had grown. Furthermore, a brand-new dot floated nearby.

Deciding what kind of TV to get, where to get it, setting it up, and determining which streaming service felt overwhelming. Hours of effort. Better to ignore it.

"We hardly watch TV any more anyway," Jeff said one Monday evening while we watched the two dots hover like flies over Rachel Maddow's shoulder.

We'd listened for years to friends and family talk about *Game of Thrones*, *Shrinking*, *The Perfect Couple*, *Succession*, *Yellowstone*, *The Diplomat*, and *Bridgerton* without having any idea what they were talking about. My veterinarian husband and I were completely up to date on *All Creatures Great and Small*, but no one seemed interested in discussing any shocking plot twists on that.

"You're still on cable?" one of my friends said, in surprise, when I mentioned ditching the dish. It felt similar to when I was a child and thought no one liked me because they didn't come over but then realized that much was explained by the fact that we were the only family in the neighborhood who still had a black and white TV. Becoming like our parents is a real thing, I guess.

On Black Friday, after hours of research, we found one marked down by $300. Delivery and installation, coincidentally, was $299.

"Let's do it ourselves," Jeff said.

"Yeah, okay," I said, breaking into a sweat. First, I measured the back of our car to make sure the TV would fit. Check. At the box store, the staff loaded the TV, and once home, we were relieved how light it was, and how easy to carry from the garage into our living room.

Text update to our kids: "Operation New TV, Phase One: Successfully inside." They responded with many laughing emojis.

The directions for hooking it up, surprisingly, only showed three connections. Plus, our OCD tendencies were mollified by getting rid of all those cable cords.

Text update to kids: "Operation New TV, Phase Two: Successfully hooked up." They responded with surprised emojis.

Now, could we figure out how to watch a program? Which streaming service carried the few TV programs that we watched? Needed: a spreadsheet.

After extensive research, using our new remote, we signed in and tested to see if we could actually watch the promised programs.

Dare I observe that watching a LIVE program—as easy as punching a button in the 70's—has become much more difficult? This existential difference between cable and streaming was hard for us to grasp.

"We both have post-graduate degrees!" Jeff yelled as our daughter, Caitlin, coached us on using the remote. "How can it be so hard to tape a TV show?"

"Dad, you don't need to tape programs. You watch the shows whenever you want."

"They don't play golf whenever I decide to watch," Jeff argued. "They have tee-times."

It seemed that we could watch plenty of recorded golf *after* it had been played.

"But isn't the point to watch it *while* it's being played?" Jeff insisted. Live sports now appear to be "special events" that you have to pay for. "I can't figure this out." Jeff tossed the remote to me after messing with it for an hour. "You try."

I punched button after button, painstakingly input the titles of programs using that archaic alphabetical system and ended up in some endless inescapable loop.

"We saw this before. This is not it."

"Fine, you try it!" I lobbed the remote back. Trying to navigate this stuff gives me such a headache, I gave up and read a book. Hours later, we figured out how to watch live news, golf tournaments, and Netflix. All was well until friends staying overnight on their way to Florida wanted to watch *New Year's Rockin' Eve*.

After I spent an hour typing it in without success, our friend grabbed the remote and shouted into it. "New Year's Rockin' Eve!"

"You can talk to it?" I said.

Then we tossed the remote from one to another and each tried until we were ready to scream. But no amount of typing, talking, or shouting turned up *New Year's Rockin' Eve*, until I Googled it and found out it was a "special event" to be paid for separately.

Mission impossible!

We wished each other "Happy New Year," and retired to our respective bedrooms at 10:15. While 2024 is in the record books, Operation New TV is ongoing.

We still haven't found *All Creatures Great and Small*. And we wonder, *was that strange black dot really that bad?* •

Copyright 2025, Lisa Williams Kline

Lisa Williams Kline is the author of two award-winning novels for adults, *Between the Sky and the Sea* and *Ladies' Day*, as well as an essay collection entitled *The Ruby Mirror* and a short story collection entitled *Take Me*. She lives in Davidson with her veterinarian husband, a cat who can open doors, and a sweet chihuahua who has played Bruiser Woods in *Legally Blonde: The Musical*.

We Thought We Were Safe Here
by Beth Bixby Davis

Until Hurricane Helene slammed through the Southern Appalachian Mountains in late September 2024, leaving massive death and destruction in her wake, we felt relatively safe in our home. Not anymore.

While living in Western North Carolina for decades, and in our current rural home in Fletcher for 46 years, I felt the comfort of a giant hug, being surrounded by these beautiful Blue Ridge Mountains. Being away from coastal flooding, western wildfires, southwest droughts, and northern frigid temperatures, felt like we had the perfect location. Apparently, a lot of others felt the same because the number of people moving and retiring here has been substantial. Of course, we had some previous flooding and the Blizzard of '93 was tragic, but we were able to bounce back into our normal lives each time.

On Thursday, September 26, we heard a storm was coming, and made some preparations. I went to the grocery store and bought some supplies, adding soups, luncheon meats, bread and drinks, preparing for a possible short power outage. I drew some drinking water and had two pails of flushing water sitting in the bathtub.

My garden had hundreds of giant zinnias blooming, and

I meant to cut them, but it started raining before I got around to do it. The rain was heavy, and my husband measured eight inches in his rain gauge. Still, we weren't too concerned, but the ground was getting saturated causing the tree roots to be unstable, and we live in the woods.

At 4:00 a.m. Friday morning our power went out, and I remember saying "I guess it has started." The rain was beating down in sheets against our windows and the wind howled in bursts of frantic screams. We knew we were in trouble. We could hear trees crashing down and when it was daylight, we watched from our patio door as more trees continued to fall.

It was terrifying to be living in the woods as the torrential hurricane rain poured down. The wind blasted gusts that laid down majestic oaks like they were toothpicks. We closed blinds to protect us from broken glass if the windows should break. Watching the tall trees sway outside the high windows in our room with the cathedral ceiling was heart-stopping.

I remember saying, "We should hurry and get dressed and put some heavy boots on in case a tree falls on the house and we have to evacuate," and so we did.

We watched the nearby creek rising, crossing the cornfield, then crossing our driveway. We worried it might reach the garage. We watched our garden and my zinnias disappear as blocks of firewood floated by.

At about 10 a.m. we heard a loud knocking on our door. Our young neighbor was checking on us. He reported that our driveway was blocked by too many trees to count and that he had waded through four feet of water in our driveway. He was soaked to the skin, tall boots full of water and worried about what he would find when he got here. We assured him we were okay and the house okay, so far. What a thoughtful young man to have as a neighbor. His family- wife, 2-year- old and newborn baby, were safe also.

The rain paused about noon on Friday, and we donned boots and raincoats to survey damage. Too many trees down to count. A tree landed on our barn and others leveled our riding ring. The trees were too thick and intertwined for us to get through to see how far up our long driveway was blocked. It was still very windy and too dangerous to be out, so we went back to the house.

We tried to be brave, thankful that we were safe and that our house, garage and vehicles were unharmed. But the sadness we felt after all the decades we worked to make our 11 acres of this earth a beautiful haven to spend our retirement, was deep. Many people who visit us for the first time say, "You are so lucky to live here in the privacy of these woods."

We soon started to hear that our beautiful, quaint and artsy Asheville was much destroyed. The death and destruction from the hurricane and accompanying tornadoes in Western North Carolina remain overwhelming. The pictures of the places we know and love are heart breaking. Nothing will ever be the same. The clean-up and rebuilding will take years and billions of dollars. *Where will people live, how will they survive this loss?* We are blessed to be retired and to have just trees, brush, and giant root balls to worry about.

After 17 days, we have power and water for which we are grateful. Still, my heart is heavy for what others are going through. Trying to be optimistic, we hope all will recover. •

Copyright 2025, Beth Bixby Davis

Beth Bixby Davis was born in Northern New York and moved to the Asheville area of North Carolina in the mid-1960's where she reared her family, raised Arabian horses and had a 30-year career in nursing. Enjoying a hobby of writing, she recently published a second book of short stories, essays and poetry, called *Patchwork Collection Volume II*. Her creative nonfiction work has appeared in previous PSPP collections as well as on the podcast, "6-minute Stories." In a writing class through OLLI at UNC-Asheville, she contributed two fictional pieces which were published in *Stories To Go*. She belongs to Talespinners Writers Group.

If We Could Just Get Married
by Lorraine Martin Bennett

I always suspected my soon-to-be-husband decided to marry me when he learned we had purchased the same make and model car on our meager cub reporter salaries at the old *Atlanta Journal*. His was a red Chevrolet Chevelle, straight transmission. Mine was navy blue, automatic transmission. Except for color and transmission, the cars were identical. But my payments were lower. I believe he decided then and there I might be a smart catch.

Because we would be living together and working in the same office (he in sports, me in news) we decided we would only need one vehicle, therefore one car payment. He gave his car to his brother. We planned a December wedding in my hometown in the western North Carolina mountains. His task was to drive to the town on his day off, complete marriage license requirements, return to the city, and pick me up at the end of my 3:30 p.m. shift at the newspaper.

At the appointed time, I waited. And waited. And waited. This was before cellphones, so I could not track him down and learn why he was late. After a half hour, I decided he had been detained. I took the city bus to the small apartment we had just rented. At that time, it contained my bedroom furniture, his television set, and that was all.

In the apartment I continued to wait. And wait. And wait. Our phone had not been installed at that point. About 8 o'clock I decided I had paced enough worry steps across the bare floor. I would find a pay phone and call my parents to learn when he might have left the town for the city.

Just as I was about to walk out the door, I heard a tentative knock. To my great joy and relief, my fiancé was standing just beyond the threshold.

"I'm in trouble," he said, barely looking me in the eye. "I drove your car off a mountain."

He had, in fact, attempted to pass a pickup truck on a rain-slickened two-lane road—on *Blood Mountain*, no less. He later told me how eerie was the feeling as the car skidded off the road, went over the shoulder (no guard rail), trundled down the mountain between trees and came to rest against a sapling. During his impromptu ride, the radio continued to play merry Christmas music.

He was uninjured, not a scratch, but his pride was badly damaged. The undercarriage of the car was not unscathed however, but it was repairable. He hitched a ride into Atlanta with a friendly and sympathetic motorist. A few days later we hired a wrecker and had the car pulled up the mountainside and taken for repairs.

The day before the wedding my intended arrived bringing the wedding cake from Atlanta. He was driving a brand new, rented Plymouth Fury with every available gadget and gizmo.

On the drive home from the evening rehearsal, the car stalled in the middle of the road. Wouldn't move an inch. The too many "bells and whistles" had exhausted the battery.

For our quick honeymoon trip to Gatlinburg, Tennessee, we borrowed my father's car.

That was only the beginning of our misadventures. After we had parked my dad's car and spent our first glorious newly-wedded night at the Sidney James Motel (no longer in existence, but just $10, I believe) we discovered my husband's grandmother, who had come from Alabama to attend our wedding, had left her winter coat in the back seat of the car. To this day, no one has been able to tell me just how it came to be there.

We were due back at our respective jobs in *two* days. No mercy was given to two mostly broke kids trying to start two new careers *and* a new marriage.

Back home in our tiny one-bedroom apartment on Briarcliff Road in Atlanta, we had neither washer nor dryer in the unit. We trudged a couple of blocks to a coin-operated laundry to wash our essentials. One cold afternoon we left the clothes in the dryer while we ran a few errands. When we returned, no clothes. *What could any thief possibly want with damp underwear?*

Months and years later, long after the car's undercarriage was successfully repaired and the missing clothing replaced, we would laugh about our misadventures during that long December.

If We Could Just Get Married

Did they cement our marriage and prepare us for the twists and turns of decades together when my husband faced many health challenges? Did they give us a framework for coping with the ordeals waiting in our future?

I believe they did. We lasted 54 years, until I lost him in 2020. •

Copyright 2025, Lorraine Martin Bennett

Lorraine Martin Bennett is a print, web and broadcast journalist from Murphy, North Carolina, who graduated with her high school journalism medal and received a scholarship to UNC Chapel Hill. Her reporting career includes the Atlanta Journal, Los Angeles Times, and, in retirement, the Clay County Progress. She worked as assignment editor, news writer, copy editor, producer, and editorial manager before ending her career at CNN International. Her two published novels, *Cat on a Black Moon*, and *Darla*, are available on Amazon, Kindle, Barnes & Noble and other websites. A third novel is in the works.

Unseen Troubles
by Marcia J. Wick

My sister and I, four years apart in age, each inherited an eye disease that causes the insidious loss of sight. Back in the early 1990s, when we were in our 30s, our daytime vision was still functional, but we were nearly blind in the dark. Together, we traveled from Denver to Boston to participate in a study of retinal degenerative diseases at the Massachusetts Eye and Ear Infirmary.

For two full days, we tolerated rigorous eye exams requiring constant dilation of our pupils. We were subjected to prolonged periods of adaptation to the dark, after which we were expected to stare without blinking at a barrage of flickering lights. Specialized contact lenses were affixed under our eyelids. They were wired to a computer that recorded the electrical response of our retinas to the stimulus. The wires were taped to our foreheads and cheeks, restricting our movements lest the lenses pop out. If that happened, the technician would have to restart the torturous test from the beginning.

Desperate to help the researchers find a treatment or a cure for our progressive vision loss, we endured the discomfort without complaint. (Okay, we did grumble some in the privacy of our hotel room at night, but we were doing our part for science.)

After two days of this agony, my sister and I were determined to enjoy our final evening in Boston, famous for its lobster restaurants on the wharf. We deserved an expensive night out on the town for our trouble, we agreed.

We started walking but were overtaken by pouring rain. We managed to hail a cab a block away from our hotel. We sported dark sunglasses in the taxi even though it was night. The harsh headlights of moving cars and the bright streetlights reflecting off the wet pavement would have pierced our dilated pupils like laser beams. No matter those problems or that our clothes were drenched and our feet sloshed in our shoes, nothing would deter us from enjoying our well-earned evening out.

Despite the nasty weather, heavy traffic, dripping hair, and weary eyeballs, we cheered like schoolgirls when we arrived at the restaurant in time for our reservation. We removed our sunglasses as the doorman ushered us into the popular establishment. Guests were packed shoulder to shoulder in the dimly lit lobby. After checking in at the front counter, we stood frozen in place, unable to navigate with low vision through the crowd. White canes would have helped, but we were not yet ready to admit we needed the recognizable mobility aids that would have signaled to others our challenge.

Two lovely ladies rescued us, inviting us to share their table at the bar while we awaited our turn to dine. So far so good. We patted each other on the back and bragged about reaching our destination without incident. We ordered wine all around and chatted until our names were announced.

"Follow me," the host instructed.

Our guide took off at full speed and was engulfed by the cavernous restaurant like Jonah swallowed by the whale. My sister and I linked arms and forged ahead, hoping to catch up with our host. Weaving like drunks, even though we'd only consumed one glass of wine each, we bounced like pinballs through the dark maze of dinner tables and occupied chairs.

"Excuse me," I apologized again and again. "I'm sorry," my sister echoed as we bumped into several irritated diners.

With a shriek, I collided into our host waiting impatiently in the shadow of a soft light decorating the center of our assigned table. My sister and I groped clumsily for our chairs and sat heavily with a huge sigh of relief. We clapped palms acknowledging our success with a high five.

"Here are your menus." We waved our arms in the air and fumbled for the weighty bill of fare.

"Please, enjoy your meal," said the host before disappearing.

We had been left alone to decipher the lengthy list of selections. With our hands, we explored the menu's elegant cover embossed in silver foil.

Salivating, we began perusing the oversized menu, but our dream of lobster drenched in lemon butter suddenly soured— it was as if the menu had been printed in invisible ink. Ash-gray script swirled across the textured buff pages like hazy clouds crossing the sky at dusk.

We disintegrated into laughter. After overcoming one obstacle after another, we had run into a brick wall—we simply could not read the menu.

When the waiter appeared and asked for our order, we replied in resigned unison, "What do you recommend?"

Ultimately, we enjoyed a nice bottle of chardonnay along with lobster tails that the chef kindly shelled for us, setting aside the bitter lemon wedges we surely would not have seen.

More than 30 years later, without a treatment or cure for our progressive vision loss, we've learned to rely on assistive technology and ask for help when needed to avoid embarrassment and unseen troubles. •

Copyright 2025, Marcia J. Wick

Marcia J. Wick is a blind, grey-haired grandmother retired from a professional writing career. She writes freelance if it pays, for fun if not. Her work has appeared in the *Motherwell* blog, *Chicken Soup for the Soul*, *Modern Dog Magazine*, *Guide Dogs for the Blind Alumni News*, and *Magnets and Ladders*, published online by Behind Our Eyes, an organization for writers with disabilities. Her essays reflect on parenting, caregiving, living with a disability, and adventures with her guide dog. When not reading or writing, Marcia volunteers and enjoys the outdoors with family and friends. Contact her at marciajwick@gmail.com.

Not a Suitable Suitor
by Suzanne Cottrell

While playing in our backyard on a June morning, my three siblings and I approached Mitzi's kennel. She stood at the gate, wagged her tail, and waited for pats on her head. My youngest brother David tugged on my shirtsleeve and pointed. "Look, what's that?"

Having found a dead rabbit at the fence line last week, I hesitated and swallowed hard. Specks of fresh blood but no sign of a carcass. David sprinted toward the house. "Mitzi's hurt!"

Our dad bounded from the porch and hustled to Mitzi's kennel. "Where's she hurt?"

My other two siblings and I shrugged our shoulders and raised our hands with palms up. Dad entered her pen and rubbed his hands over her body. Afterward, his furrowed brow smoothed, and he grinned. "Mitzi's in heat." He would make breeding arrangements with a registered purebred English Pointer in Illinois, a five-and-a-half-hour drive from our house in Oxford, Ohio. Dad and Mitzi had made the trip two times before, without success.

Because Mitzi moved slower then, and her keen sense of smell had lessened, Dad dreamed of training one of Mitzi's offspring and hunting for pheasant and quail. He planned to keep one puppy and sell the rest to cover the stud fee and make some money. Mitzi, his well-schooled, working bird dog represented artistry in motion. Beholding her on point, you'd see she posed gracefully with her front right leg raised and bent. From her snout to the tip of her tail, she was an arrow honed on its target. Her short, cream fur with liver-colored spots provided camouflage in the grain fields. Alert, focused, and on command, Mitzi flushed birds into the air. After Dad made a successful shot, she retrieved the ring-necked pheasant, gently mouthed the bird, and dropped him at his boots.

Even though he assured us her kennel was secure, Dad directed us to help keep any male dogs away. That afternoon our neighbors' Boston terrier and their standard short-haired dachshund dashed along the six-foot high chain-link fence. Mitzi barked, poked her nose through the fence, and sniffed her wooers. We shooed them away, but they were persistent. The metal fence wavered when they pawed and tried to climb it. We shouted and clapped but only dissuaded them by spraying them with water from the garden hose.

Two days later, we alerted Dad to a small mound of dirt piled by a corner fence post, but we saw no sign of entry into Mitzi's kennel. He kicked the dirt. When he cussed, we covered our ears and bolted to the far side of the backyard. The two male dogs darted into the boxwood bushes. "Time to move Mitzi to the basement," Dad declared.

On Saturday morning, Mom spread worn towels on the back seat of the station wagon. After opening the passenger door, Dad tapped on the seat. "Come on, girl." Mitzi climbed onto the seat. As soon as he closed the door, Mitzi pressed her nose against the window. "See you in a couple of days." We waved as he backed the car down the driveway.

Monday evening, Dad and Mitzi returned home. As the weeks passed, Mitzi's nipples enlarged, and she napped most of the day. As Mitzi's midsection grew, Dad hummed and whistled merry tunes around the house.

A month later, Mitzi delivered six puppies. Four were chocolate brown, but two had a white chest blaze and stocking paws. When the vet said their spots will appear later, Dad rubbed his chin; Mom cast her eyes downward and shook her head. The puppies had Mitzi's head shape, but short legs supported their elongated bodies. Grandpa Jennings teased our dad he'd have to tie flags on their tails if he took them bird hunting, so he'd be able to see them among the wheat shafts. Dad grimaced. My siblings and I didn't care what the puppies looked like. They were puppies!

"Can we keep one?" I asked. Dad bellowed a firm *no*.

A few weeks later, my siblings and I darted around the backyard, pursued by six yipping and yapping puppies that nipped at our ankles. Mom sipped iced tea and gazed from the back porch while Dad recorded our antics with the video camera. When we tumbled to the ground, we shielded our faces from licks as we giggled. One puppy snatched Rob's baseball cap and darted under a bush. "Hey, come back here."

Dad's laugh disguised his disappointment. He sold three puppies and gave three away, including one to Grandpa

Not a Suitable Suitor

Jennings. Grandpa let us name her Brownie. When quail season arrived, Grandpa consoled Dad. "Brownie may not be a bird dog, but she's a fine squirrel and rabbit dog," adding with a laugh, "—even without a tail flag."

Dad patted Brownie on the head. "Guess that's some consolation." •

Copyright 2025, Suzanne Cottrell

Suzanne Cottrell, a member of the Taste Life Twice Writers and NC Writers' Network, lives with her husband in rural Granville County, NC. An outdoor enthusiast and retired teacher, she enjoys reading, writing, knitting, hiking, Pilates, and belly dancing. Her prose has appeared in numerous journals and anthologies, including the Personal Story Publishing Project, Inwood Indiana Press, Quillkeepers Press, and *Parks and Points*. She's the author of three poetry chapbooks: *Gifts of the Seasons, Autumn and Winter*; *Gifts of the Seasons, Spring and Summer*; and *Scarred Resilience*; and *Nature Calls Outside My Window, A Collection of Poems and Stories*. www.suzanneswords.com

Four-minute Showers
by Dawn McCormack

"Mommy... Can I have some juice?"

"Not now, Megan," I grimaced, as my 5-year-old tugged on the shower curtain. "Just another minute or so. Go ahead now; drink your milk. I'll pour you some juice as soon as I'm done."

"But Mom-m-my!"

"Megan, I said I'll be right out!" I answered, trying not to sound as frustrated as I felt. "Go back into the living room and let me finish!"

She hesitated for a moment, as if trying to make up her mind whether she should argue. Then the shower curtain relaxed, and I breathed a sigh of relief. Round One to me!

But my illusion of tranquility was shattered, and, anxious, I hurried up, frantically trying to rinse shampoo out of my hair, knowing she'd be returning for Round Two at any moment. *Shower in peace!?* Not likely. Those words held no meaning for a single mother of a 5-year-old.

No, life wasn't always like this. Just for a moment my mind

flashed back to those luxurious, pre-baby, 40-minute baths, complete with aromatic candles and bubbles, when I'd read and daydream and actually *relax*. How much I had taken for granted; and how much I had yet to learn! Now I had to plan and scheme for just a few free minutes. And even then…

I thought I'd worked it out so perfectly this time: *Sesame Street* on TV; a full cup of milk, complete with bendy-straw, of course; and, best of all: her brand new *Etch A Sketch*. *Guaranteed* to keep her spellbound for at least ten full minutes! Or so I'd thought…

"Mommy…"

My thoughts snapped back to the present as she tugged on the curtain again.

"I'm almost done," I promised, snatching the green vinyl barrier back into place, but not in time to stop a spray of water from cascading out onto the bathroom floor.

"I cleaned it up, Mommy."

Cleaned it up?, I thought.

"Cleaned *what* up?!" I burbled, shampoo dribbling down over my eyes and into my mouth. "MEG-AN!?"

But she'd already retreated by the time I was able to see again, leaving me in a panic and hastily rinsing out the remaining shampoo.

I cleaned it up spun through my mind, and I groaned as visions of everything from ketchup-smudged rugs to de-potted plants assaulted me.

Knowing I'd better finish quickly, I jumped out of the shower, most likely still sporting half a bottle of shampoo. Then, taking a quick stab at drying off, I threw on my old blue robe, and dashed into the living room.

There she sat at her little snack-table, still watching her show, playing with her *Etch A Sketch*, and drinking her juice. *Juice?*

"Megan…?" Her name hung in the air as I started backing toward the kitchen. "I thought I told you to wait for me to get you some juice…"

"I got it. All. By. Myself," she responded with pride, adding as she followed me to the scene of her accomplishment, "I cleaned it up."

"Right."

The single word stuck in my throat as I surveyed the disaster before me: Near-empty plastic pitcher—recently full of apple juice—lying on its side on the edge of the counter, still dripping its remains onto the cabinet below. Sticky, wet dish towel bunched halfway into the sink. One small ocean of apple juice had been swabbed over the entire kitchen floor. (Washed yesterday, of course.)

"Oh, Megan!" I announced, gritting my teeth as my bare feet squinched their way across the gooey tiles. "I told you to wait!"

"I cleaned it up," she repeated, reminding me of her defense.

As my gaze travelled from the floor to the soggy dishtowel and back to her big, blue, imploring eyes, I realized how hard she *had* tried.

"All right, honey," I sighed, giving her a hug as my anger subsided. "I know you did. And you did a good job. But next time, wait until I'm out of the shower, Okay, Megan…?"

But she had already gone, back to her juice, TV, and *Etch A Sketch*, leaving me to continue *my* job of being the single mother of a 5-year-old.

"Oh well," I sighed. As I reached for the paper towels, I glanced at the clock to realize I was in the shower for fewer than five minutes. *Not even five minutes!* In that short time, she'd managed to accomplish what would take me half an hour to undo!

A grateful smile soon crept onto my face. I knew it could have been much worse. At least I'd gotten out of the shower when I did! With a shudder, I wondered what might have happened if I'd stayed in long enough to use the conditioner, too! •

Copyright 2025, Dawn McCormack

Dawn McCormack, a former Spanish teacher, resides in Plainfield, Connecticut. She has been writing for many years. Short story credits include "Columbus Single Scene" and "The Storyteller." While she is currently working on a middle-grade book, she has also had considerable success with her poetry in several publications, including *The Avocet* (nature), *Exit 13* (travel), *The Lyric* (general), and *Illumen* (speculative). For speculative writing, she frequently draws upon her dreams.

Fire and Rain
by Kristen T. Bryson

Recently, I suggested to my husband that a new car might be in order given the age and accumulated mileage on my vehicle. Since our two kids had chosen in-state public universities, we could now afford the car of my dreams, a 2021 Range Rover, Byron Blue with ivory interior, a V8 engine and long wheelbase. After researching for several days, my husband located my dream car at a Las Vegas dealership, and we excitedly proceeded with the purchase and requisite insurance.

Because we live in North Carolina, the dealership recommended a broker to arrange for a transport trailer service to bring the car east. We explained that delivery to Charlotte needed to occur after our planned trip to Boone for our son's Family Weekend at Appalachian State University. The broker lined up a driver with delivery anticipated just after our return home. Although we were told we would receive photos of the car being loaded, we only received one of the trailer taken from afar. With the dealer's assurance that our car was indeed on this trailer, off we went to Boone, with fingers crossed for the delivery of my dream car.

We left for Boone after work on Thursday evening. The rain had been heavy that day, and we knew that Hurricane Helene was tracking for western North Carolina. We naively believed that by Saturday, the storm would have passed, and we could enjoy game day with our son. The drive began smoothly, until our progress was impeded by a downed power line across Highway 321. Our attempts to detour around the impasse proved futile, so we overnighted there in Hickory, intending to continue up the mountain in the daylight.

The next morning saw winds and heavy rain, but we decided to keep going, albeit very slowly. We reached the outskirts of Boone before water began accumulating on the roadway in low areas, requiring detours and careful navigation. We managed to get within a half mile of our Airbnb before encountering water on the road deep enough to prevent us from continuing. We sought temporary refuge at a nearby McDonald's, smartly choosing the parking space with the highest elevation. *Safe*, we thought.

Within moments of walking in the door, an employee shouted that anyone parked in the back lot needed to immediately move their car because the creek was flooding. One young woman ran outside, and we watched as she climbed into her car through the trunk because the water was rising so quickly. Amazingly, she got the car started and was able to move it to an inclined portion of the lot. At that point, we realized that all the adjacent streets were flooding, and we appeared to be stranded on "McDonald's Island." My mind ran wild, and I imagined us having to climb to the roof for safety, waving wildly and awaiting rescue, like so many storm images on the news. As we watched cars being swept down the street, I remember thinking that even if we lost this car, at least a new one would arrive in two days.

Fortunately, the manager allowed us to shelter in place until conditions improved. For four hours, we chatted and slid around surprisingly slippery floors. When the rain let up, we used alternate directions to our Airbnb and finally reached our destination. Within minutes of walking into our rental, we lost power and water. However, we were thrilled to reach our son and visit; we spent the night and returned home the next day. Our power was out in Charlotte, too.

We were sitting at the kitchen table playing Rummikub by candlelight when the phone rang. We heard the woman on the line, from the transport company, say, "I've never had to make a call like this before, but the trailer carrying your car burned up while traveling through Texas. It is a total loss. I'm so sorry, but I don't yet know much about the incident." She paused while we took in the news, then asked, "Do you have any questions?"

My husband, shocked and bewildered, simply replied, "No, I guess not," at which point I interjected, "Well, I have questions! We need more details." With what she told us, we spoke to police and fire departments, insurance companies, and adjusters. We learned the trailer was also carrying a Ferrari, a Lamborghini, a Porsche, and two classic cars. We stared in disbelief at the photograph of a pile of ashes, all that remained of my dream car. And then we felt grateful. Significant tragedy and destruction occurred in western North Carolina during those couple of days. We were safe and well and, after all, it was just a car. Nevertheless, my resigned acceptance over the possible loss of a car expressed at "McDonald's Island" turned out to be a good bit optimistic. I don't know if I tempted fate, but I sure counted my chickens. •

Fire and Rain

Copyright 2025, Kristen T. Bryson

Kristen T. Bryson lives in Charlotte, North Carolina, and this is her first writing submission for publication. She was encouraged by a family friend to share her story. She has been inspired by her father-in-law's commitment to writing his memoirs and an extensive compilation of letters to his grandchildren, and she hopes to continue the family legacy of writing stories that preserve her family's history.

With a Lump in My Throat
by Marion Cohen

For 14 years, I was employed as a high school mathematics teacher. I enjoyed my career, had wonderful rapport with my students, and was involved in extracurricular activities. My professional work life was quite satisfying.

Another factor that made my days so pleasing was that I had become romantically involved with another member of the faculty. Although we had a complicated relationship, I was quite head over heels with this man. After a few years of this romantic struggle, I thought it was in my best interest to extricate myself from the situation. Seeing this man, every day was affecting many aspects of my life. Even our mutual colleagues observed the tension that ensued between us.

Ironically, during that low time of my life, I received a phone call from a department head from another district asking if I'd like to transfer schools. He was seeking to fill an opening and had received a glowing recommendation about my talents as an educator.

On a lark, I decided to go on the interview. This other school was quite impressive, and this affluent suburban school enjoyed many more advantages than the school where I had been employed. The principal who interviewed me was quite impressed with my resume, my references, and I was offered the position on the spot, giving me the coming weekend to decide.

I had drawbacks to consider, as well. I'd be giving up my tenured position. Also, I would be losing the 85 sick days I had accumulated.

The plus side was that I would no longer be exposed to the emotional turmoil of seeing the man I was still in love with, day in and day out, as our relationship had come to its unfortunate end. Also, the buildings and campus of this new school, in general, were far better equipped, and I could imagine that my teaching responsibilities would be more interesting, as this school was academically superior to where I was presently employed. When I toured the school along with my new perspective department head, I was so taken by the physical building and how well it was maintained. The mathematics department had its own office where staff had a desk, filing cabinet, shelves for books, and a coffee machine percolating throughout the day. The most luxurious aspect of this facility was a restroom situated next door to the department office. Quite literally, I thought I died and went to teaching heaven, as in my present school there was only one faculty restroom, a long walk from my classroom.

I returned home after the interview and spent the weekend contemplating this career change. Professionally, I would be giving up a lot, tenure, 17 weeks of accumulated sick days, and most importantly, my already earned professional reputation. I would need to prove myself once again to an entirely new staff. The upside was that along with all the enhanced advantages this new school offered, I assumed my emotional stress would wane during each passing week as I would no longer be near the man with whom I'd been passionately entangled.

The weekend ended, and I made my decision. I presented my letter of resignation and accepted the new position starting the following month. The adjustment to my new classes was effortless, and the students were very cooperative. Slowly, I was meeting members of the faculty, happily acclimating to all the incredible advantages this new working environment provided. I was impressed at how much easier the workload was at this school. Although I missed my former colleagues, I just kept working every day, knowing I would adjust.

A few months later, my entire perspective changed. During a class discussion, as my hand touched my neck awaiting a response from a student, I felt a lump alongside my neck. That afternoon I was on my way to my internist's office. After many tests, I was diagnosed with thyroid cancer. Necessary surgery removed the gland, and in the process, one of my vocal cords was severed causing temporary loss of the projection of my much-needed vocal capacity. I was immediately on medical leave without pay as I had lost my sick days when I transferred school districts. I was also non-tenured which was problematic as well.

The wisdom of my decision to transfer schools certainly was now in question as I struggled financially to maintain my lifestyle during my recovery. Had I remained in my former position, my sick days would surely have covered my extended absence. I had been attracted to all the trappings of the new facility and to escaping my relationship problems. Looking back, what I did not consider more seriously was my security.

It was a lesson learned for sure. But how do we know, when do we know, if what glitters will prove to be gold? When do we just swallow hard and take our chances? •

Copyright 2025, Marion Cohen

Born in Brooklyn, New York, Marion Cohen spent three decades as a mathematics educator before turning to writing. Her three novels and two short story collections focus on characters whose strong connections reflect a variety of emotions such as love, admiration, and courage. Ms. Cohen's essays have appeared in various online magazines and journals. Presently residing in Cherry Hill, New Jersey, Ms. Cohen also enjoys working on exquisite needlepoint projects, such as displayed on the cover of her recent short story collection, *Words While Resting on My Pillows*.

Tequila or Not Tequila
by Jeanne VanBuren

There we were, late afternoon in December 2000, redhead and blond sisters, riding on the local bus, *Corazon Dorado*, with our precious tote filled with two reds, one white, and one rosé. My sister Chris and I were riding past cinder block homes, rustic farms with goats and chickens and far from any developed part of the supposedly walkable city of Mazatlán, Mexico. The roads were devolving from paved to gravel to dirt as we were panicking in silence about how we became the only remaining bus passengers parking in a grassy field at the end of anywhere recognizable. Our money-saving adventure was spoiled by our realization that not all buses eventually return to the depot.

Our vacation was a college graduation treat for my sister during a timeshare bonus week at a "quaint," high-rise resort in Mazatlán. The resort was not an all-inclusive venue. It had a kitchenette, two bathrooms, two beds, and fans for air conditioning. The complex had four different swimming pools, lush greenery and a questionable bar. We packed warm weather essentials, first aid kit, and *Imodium* as a precaution of a temperamental digestive system if we drank Mexico's water. We arrived late in the evening for a *real* vacation with no specific plans except to see and do whatever we were in the mood for. We were two competent but naive travelers missing a Spanish-English dictionary.

I don't remember what or if we had dinner on our first night, however we did find the way to "the bar." I prefer wine; I am not a tequila drinker nor a beer drinker. But Chris is an "any drinker," primed to celebrate her recent achievement. When in Mexico, tequila is a given, wine, apparently, is not. When I inquired *what do you have in red?* the bartender poured a half glass of some random red wine dragged from underneath. When that bottle ran out, he then proceeded to blow dust off another random bottle to make a full glass. It wasn't a Cabernet, Merlot, or Shiraz, it was just red—two blended reds from the leftovers of two questionable bottles. So, the first task for the next day was our quest for a real, sealed bottle of wine—or two.

Without a car, our options to acquire provisions were by foot, by *pulmonia,* or by public transportation. We nixed walking because most places were *not* within walking distance. Besides, hiking was not on our agenda. *Pulmonia* are gas-powered, open-air taxis similar to golf carts and cost about $6 per person. The bus stopped almost in front of the resort and ran about $0.35 to ride. We picked the least expensive option and the most public-safety-in-numbers selection. We chose the *Corazon de la Ciudad* bus heading towards the city.

We got off the bus at a tourist section overlooking the cliffs. A kid there was crowing the talents of the "brave cliff divers." After he collected enough donations from the viewing crowd, he would signal his partner to dive. I noticed they eventually split the money for their shared spectacle. A few such spectacles later, we wandered around the city to find a worthier wine and some lunch. We took our self-guided tour, checking out bull fighting arenas, historic churches, and stores noting times to return if desired. When the time came to head back, we were disoriented and unsure which direction to return to our hotel base. Believing whole-heartedly that all buses eventually go back to the depot, we hopped on any bus, marked *Corazon Dorado* (Golden Heart) thinking it was *Corazon de la Ciudad* (Heart of the city) to return us to enjoy the remainder of the day and my purchased wine.

We paid our fare and watched locals get on and get off; but none of the scenery looked familiar. More people departed, no more locals or tourists boarded, and the roads were getting rougher. We never made it back to any place that resembled a depot. Eventually the bus stopped in a dusty remote field and the driver turned off his engine. Apparently, bus drivers take their breaks in that grassy field. The driver had completed his route and was indifferent to two stranded passengers. After the shock of our flawed thinking sank in, we conveyed through hand gestures our desired destination. Luckily for us, another bus driver who was finished with his break drove us back to a strip mall-ish place and gave us transfer instructions to the correct *"Corazon"* to complete our outing.

When we made it back to our resort base, ready to enjoy—in its entirety—one of the four sealed bottles, we found no corkscrew in the kitchenette. In our next travels—definitely with an accompanying language dictionary and a corkscrew—I might also take the golfcart taxi, improve my Spanish, or just learn to appreciate tequila with its screw off top. •

Tequila or Not Tequila

Copyright 2025, Jeanne VanBuren

Jeanne VanBuren lives in Winston Salem, North Carolina—by way of Chesapeake, Pittsburgh, Santa Cruz and Austin—where she is a member of North Carolina Writers Network and Triad Storytime. Her many traveling adventures to share include those across 45 states, so far, with her large family, five sons, or friends. A few distant countries add to her exploits to be compiled when not busy with her multiple DIY crafting projects. Getting published has inspired more writing. She says, "Write your life. You never know when you might be someone's lighthouse."

Dream-catching
by Jane Satchell McAllister

Wake Forest University suited me quite well. Its southern locale offered more warm, sunny days than my hometown of Baltimore, Maryland. The small student population and class sizes afforded ready opportunities to develop friendships and converse with professors. Early on, I surprised my parents, reporting home that strangers passing me on the quad waved or said, "Hello." I had learned as a child in the north not to talk to strangers. Clearly, this college environment in Winston-Salem, North Carolina, had different norms.

The existence of an intercollegiate women's volleyball team provided the icing on the cake. I joined the team as a freshman walk-on in the earliest days of Title IX, when female student athletes did not receive any funding. Playing on the team led to some of the finest experiences of my life. Not only did I meet women who became lifelong friends but shared in the thrill of winning our state and regional tournaments and becoming the first Wake Forest team to participate in a national competition.

Two of my volleyball teammates at Wake Forest University chose to spend a semester abroad at the University's house in Venice, Italy. Listening to their stories of adventures and misadventures, I appreciated their bravery in pursuing an experience beyond our normal studies. Not until I took an introductory course on art history did I begin to consider such an experience for myself. The possibility of seeing Renaissance art and architecture in person rather than on a page or screen intrigued me despite my lack of facility with learning foreign languages.

Pursuing a double major and playing intercollegiate volleyball in the fall semesters demanded rigorous planning for required courses, and solid academic performance was essential to maintain the academic scholarships that paid my way. Those challenges notwithstanding, I summoned up the courage to ask for details about the Study Abroad option.

The Registrar explained the program details, all of which I could accommodate with some careful planning and execution. Then she told me the price tag. A semester abroad cost $3,000 above normal tuition, not including any expenses for weekend travel that represented a major attraction of the program. That sum far exceeded my capacity at that time. I consulted with the Financial Aid office about what options might exist for assistance, but came away empty-handed, largely because the Study Abroad program had just launched a few years earlier and the University had not yet developed financial packages specific to the program. The college that fitted me so well in all other regards had placed an insurmountable barrier to a dream I dared to have. That hurt, and disappointment stayed with me for decades.

In the years after graduating from Wake Forest, I obtained master's degrees in business and library science, pursued my careers along several wandering paths, and built a wonderful home life around my husband and our rescued dogs. With some financial creativity, my spouse and I managed to vacation in San Francisco in our first year together despite student loans, car loans, and a mortgage, thanks to frequent flyer mileage and a pass for a free hotel stay. An extra bonus included crossing paths with the San Francisco 49ers and coming home, joyfully, with Joe Montana's autograph.

Each summer, we took time to travel in Europe, enjoying the deep and rich history and cultures of foreign countries. We made it to both London and Venice in those years, though for brief visits only. In Venice, I located the Wake Forest House next to the Guggenheim Museum and longingly imagined the daily lives of the students there. I could not help but think back on an incredible opportunity I had missed all those years before.

Now in retirement, our travel opportunities are greatly expanded and our shared love for discovery and learning persists. So, imagine my delight when my husband discovered an opportunity to live and study in Florence, Italy, one of my favorite travel destinations, for six weeks. Usually, I like to think for a time about our travel possibilities, but in this case, I called the next day and reserved my spot. The spring will see me living in my own apartment and walking to school each day, immersed in Renaissance Italy and learning the beautiful and wonderfully expressive Italian language. The setting is not London or Venice, it is even better suited to my mature interests. My lack of facility with language acquisition coupled with diminished hearing will no doubt provide some comical and frustrating moments, but I am old enough now to face the challenge unabashedly. Although I may lack the same energy and mental facility of my youth, I bring to bear on this new program a lifetime of perspective and experience that will enrich my time in Florence.

It took a while, but my dream is coming true.

Buona fortuna. •

Copyright 2025, Jane Satchell McAllister

Jane Satchell McAllister's writings draw inspiration from the wide variety of people and places she encounters, from her home base in Davie County, North Carolina, to rich adventures across our country and abroad. She has co-authored two Images of America books through Arcadia Publishing and served for nine years as director of the county public library. Her current writing project is compiling stories based on decades of travel, both fiction and nonfiction, almost as much fun as the trips themselves.

The Water Tower
by Annie McLeod Jenkins

P icture, if you will, two small-town girls, barely teenagers, sprawled on a double bed, idly pulling the loose threads from the chenille bedspread and pondering how they might find something exciting to do on a dull fall evening in 1962 or 1963. They were alone in the house, since the parent-in-charge, Betty's mother, was at a party; and Betty's sister was spending the night with a friend. *What could go wrong?*

As one of those girls, I can assure you that smoking and drinking, although considered daring possibilities in those innocent days, were not what we were looking for. We wanted to do something outrageous and different, something that none of our friends had attempted. The adventure we decided upon was usually the province of boys; girls of our acquaintance did not indulge in this type of foolishness. Perfect.

Being left to our own devices was nothing unusual because we were old enough to take care of ourselves. But this situation opened the door—literally—to our venturing out into the cool fall evening, hoping to find that the neighborhood was quiet and empty to accommodate our plan. And directly across Hudson Street from Betty's house was the town water tower, the site of countless assaults by teenaged fools armed with spray paint and a desire to see their names in public places.

Betty and I had no plan to leave our signatures, not being so childish as to want our names garishly displayed. And besides, this was a spontaneous decision, and we did not have any paint. We just wanted to climb the tower, like climbers have always climbed—because it was there. Our Mt. Everest.

It is at this point that my memory gets fuzzy in the details. I do recall crossing the road, sliding down the embankment, and staring up at the precariously perpendicular ladder to the top of the tower. I have no idea how we reached the bottom rung, but I do remember that it was easier said than done. The rungs were cold and damp, the night was murky, and the adventurous spirit was dying within us. On the other hand, we were not quitters. I do not recall how far we ascended but let us just say it was halfway up.

Unluckily, the night has a thousand eyes, even in small towns— or maybe especially in small towns. While we slowly, very slowly, made out way up the ladder, *someone* must have spotted us. My vote was for Margaret Elliott who lived alone on the adjacent corner and who had a notorious eagle eye. We never formally identified the squealer who called the police, but the local constabulary turned up in the form of Skippy Brown, a favorite local enforcer of the law.

Armed with a spotlight and an authoritative voice, Skippy instructed us to come down the ladder and show our faces. I must admit we were relieved that Skippy caught us, because the climb was getting harder and harder, and our desire for adventure was waning. Knowing that we were tangling with the "long arm of the law," as well as with the most benevolent, understanding, and gentle officer on the police force, we came down to face our badged nemesis.

Skippy doled out our punishment in quick succession. First, he sternly reprimanded us. Second, he "perp-walked" us up the embankment and into the back seat of his squad car. Then he hauled us off, not to the county jail, but to ponder our crimes while cruising around the sleepy community as the town clock struck the hours.

Betty and I have different memories about the squad car ride. I decidedly recall Skippy allowing us to run the siren for a brief period. She recalls that he was reluctant to take us home to an empty house, so he "baby-sat" us for the balance of his shift. This part of the story sounds like the mythical Mayberry, where Barney Fife toted his single bullet. Skippy Brown was not comedic, and Winnsboro was not always so kind; but the image does hold water.

In reflecting on this memory, I wonder how Yoda the Jedi Master would view our daring behavior. He famously pronounced "Do or do not. There is no try." Would he at least give us credit for daring the heights, even though we did not reach the top of the tower? I want to believe he would give us high marks for the idea, the effort, and the nerve. I'm also betting he would award us Junior Jedi status, in spite of the outcome of our adventure.

Thank you, Skippy, our town's "Barney" by another name.•

The Water Tower

Copyright 2025, Annie McLeod Jenkins

Annie McLeod Jenkins lives in Winston-Salem. Although she loves writing, she is frequently sidetracked by multiple other interests: choral singing, cooking, family genealogy, volunteer responsibilities, reading, fretting about the world, and trying to stay fit and healthy at age 76. She thanks the Personal Story Publishing Project for encouraging her to submit stories for this series. As usual, a good prompt stirred the pot and revealed a long-forgotten youthful escapade.

Chasing the Great Comet
by S.G. Benson

San Diego County, California, 1965.

My family lived on the corner of Draper Avenue and Fern Glen Street in a historic La Jolla home, later remodeled into a triplex. We occupied the cramped center apartment, facing both streets, and had use of a detached single-car garage. My bedroom window opened onto the adjacent apartment's front stoop.

I walked daily to the elementary school about ten blocks away. My friend, Amy, and I loved Mr. Hollenbach's sixth-grade class, where we started each morning with a current events discussion.

In October, a newly discovered cosmic snowball dominated the news. The sun-grazing Comet Ikeya-Seki, with its brilliant, 70-million-mile-long tail, created a sensation as the fourth-longest comet ever recorded.

"It should be brighter after it goes around the sun," Mr. H said, "toward the end of the month, just before daybreak."

Amy and I looked at each other and grinned. We began planning.

"We'll need to find a dark viewing spot, away from the village lights," said Amy, "and we'll have to be there by 5:00 a.m."

"Mom won't be a fan of the idea," I said. "We can't let her know what we're up to."

The night before our adventure, I checked the weather report. Often, on that part of the coast, fog rolls in during the early mornings and reduces visibility to zero. The forecast, however, called for a slight breeze and clear skies. Elated, I telephoned Amy to confirm our meet-up.

In the living room, my parents looked up from the television as I made a big show of stretching and yawning, and I started down the hallway. "I've had a long day. I'm going to bed," I said.

Mom looked surprised but waved me off.

I knew if I set my alarm, Mom would hear it, so I reasoned that going to bed early would make it easier to wake up without it. I feigned sleep when Mom peeked in later. I must have dozed off a few times, but I awoke repeatedly, shining my flashlight on the clock. The night seemed to drag on forever.

At 4 o'clock, I arose and dressed quietly. I didn't expect Mom to check on me until she called me for breakfast at 7:00. But, just in case, I stuffed a couple of coats under the covers to make the bed look occupied.

The window latch made no sound as I opened it, and I gently pushed out the screen and stepped outside onto the neighbor's porch. I shut the window behind me. The screen rattled as I replaced it, but it didn't seem to wake anyone in either apartment. I tiptoed to the garage and wheeled out my bicycle.

The morning felt chilly, and a breeze ruffled my hair. Stars shone above as I rode down Draper Avenue. No one stirred, other than a boy hunkered down on a corner under a streetlamp, putting rubber bands around newspapers for his delivery route.

Pungent salt air greeted me as I neared Amy's house by the beach. I parked my bike in her yard and tapped softly on the front door. She opened it immediately.

"Let's go," she whispered.

We started off on foot toward a bay protected by a long, unlit breakwater. During high tide, waves crashed over the seawall, sometimes hard enough to knock people off their feet. But this morning's low tide kept the cove quiet. We clambered up on the breakwater and made our way, in the dark, out to its very end. From that vantage point, we saw only a few neighborhood lights in the distance and the white line of breakers near the beach beyond the cove.

I checked my wristwatch. "It's almost time. Watch for the comet, over the hills above town."

Stars twinkled overhead as we waited. The breeze stopped and, as we continued to look up, the little points of light began to fade away.

"NOOOOO!" we shouted in unison as a fogbank crept in and swallowed the stars, one by one.

That marine layer sometimes takes until noon to lift, so I knew our adventure was doomed. Disappointed and glum, we walked back to Amy's house, and I mounted my bike to head home.

I rolled my bicycle back into the garage just at dawn. Gray mist swirled everywhere. I returned to the neighbor's porch, removed the screen, opened the window, and stepped into my bedroom, replacing the screen and closing the window behind me. I put on my pajamas, removed the "stuffing" from under the covers, and climbed into bed. My clock showed 6:45.

Mom shook me from a sound sleep at 7:00 a.m. "Wake up, Sandra. What's wrong with you? Are you feeling all right? You went to bed so early last night; I thought you'd be up by now." •

Copyright 2025, S.G. Benson

S. G. (Sandy) Benson lives in Warne, North Carolina, where she is a member of the North Carolina Writers Network-West. Her work has appeared in numerous magazines and newspapers, and she received awards from the Nebraska Press Women. She published her first book in 2021, *My Mother's Keeper: One Family's Journey Through Dementia*. Her second book, *Dear Folks: Letters Home from World War II, 1943-1946* was released in 2024. She is working on a collection of autobiographic short stories, "Girls Can't Do That." Details at https://www.sandygbenson.com/

Ride-sharing, Old School
by Barbara Mueller

Today, I would say I made some foolish choices when I was a college student during the early 70's in Buffalo, New York. But at the time and in my youth, I made choices based on my upbringing in a safe, small town of well-intentioned neighbors and acquaintances. I suppose I expected I would find the same elsewhere as well, even in college when I was away from home without wheels and often needed a ride.

During my last two years, I lived off-campus in a series of apartments. Since the first one was three miles from the university, going to classes required negotiating daily transportation. Several days a week, I rode to school with a roommate but returning home remained a challenge. Fortunately, students seeking rides gathered on a corner across from the student union and sympathetic students driving by would stop to see who might want to go in their direction.

Less predictable was making it to class on time at a satellite campus in the opposite direction. I hitchhiked there from my apartment on Niagara Falls Boulevard, a well-travelled, noisy road. Kind people stopped for a harmless-looking girl like me and I sometimes encountered the same driver repeatedly. One man who stopped for me always cautioned me about the dangers of hitchhiking in the city, but his good advice failed to diminish my naïve trust in strangers.

Returning home for holidays became another transportation problem. Most often, my parents retrieved me, a round-trip of 180 miles, but I tried to find a ride with other students when possible. The most exciting trip involved Susan, a roommate, at Christmas time. As Buffalo residents, we both had learned to ignore the weather and so we headed east on the New York State Thruway during a heavy snowstorm. Susan was an aggressive driver, and I felt some tense moments as she passed slower cars and 18-wheelers on the unplowed road in her blue Mustang. Other trips with students involved squeezing four people and all their luggage into a Volkswagen Beetle or riding in vehicles of uncertain safety-inspection status. It was adventurous—and memorable.

During my last year in college, I worked a part-time job at a local record store, a desirable job for a student The store was about five miles from the campus, so I rescued my cobwebbed childhood 3-speed bike from my parents' basement, bought a heavy chain and padlock, and found a knapsack for carrying books and a sandwich. I rode to and from that job on a busy street, the bulky chain wrapped around my hips, my long hair flying in the breeze. Enjoying the independence of having my own transportation, I pedaled home from work in the evenings as fast as I could, trying to get there before dark. To my surprise, my boyfriend complimented my muscular legs, on display below my very short skirts.

The bicycle delivered me to-and-fro until the weather changed, and the snowy, windy, 6-month Lake Erie winter arrived. A sympathetic mother of a co-worker usually brought me home from work, but getting from campus to work was still a problem. With no city bus service in that direction, I usually hitchhiked.

Catching a ride farther from campus, however, was another matter, and an education for a naive student like me. I began to encounter older male drivers of questionable character. During one memorable ride, the driver pulled over to drop me off at my destination and attempted to show me his "private parts." I scrambled out of the car without looking back. Somehow, I convinced myself that was a fluke, unlikely to happen again. So, I continued seeking rides from strangers

A few months later while leaving work, I was picked up by a man who stopped a second time to pick up two more female hitchhikers. Soon, I became aware that this driver was impaired, allowing his car to drift to the right, toward the curb. From the front passenger seat, I repeatedly leaned over to push the steering wheel to the left. He didn't even seem to notice, though I'm sure the rear-seat sisters did. As soon as he stopped at a light, I opened the door, jumped out, and slammed the door behind me, hoping the two in the back seat did the same. Relieved, I walked the rest of the way home in the dark.

After that, my confidence in strangers diminished, I decided that hitchhiking wasn't such a great idea for a girl like me. Soon enough, the school year and my job ended, and I graduated, happily—and I suppose luckily—unscathed by my hitchhiking experiences.

I left Buffalo with great expectations for my first real job. And my own car. •

Ride-sharing, Old School

Copyright 2025, Barbara Mueller

Barbara Mueller is a retired IT project manager living in Asheville, North Carolina. Her initial volunteer experience in Asheville was as a docent at the Thomas Wolfe Memorial, where she met many visitors interested in storytelling. She enjoys gardening, reading, dancing, and playing the mountain dulcimer. This is her first venture into creative non-fiction.

Taste the Disappointment
by Joe Brown

My name is Joe Brown and I'm an addict. It's been a lifelong problem that hopefully I will die with.

Oh, it's not smoking or drinking, I gave those two vices up by the time I was 12 or so. (That's a tale for another telling).

My problem is that I am addicted to eating! Not that I eat to the excess, it's just that there's almost no food that I don't like.

There was a time when I only had one food on my menu, and I got along just fine with that also. I was told that as a young person my family went to a fish fry. Once I got a taste of fried Cat Fish, I was hooked. Mom said that it took two of them pulling the meat off the bones to keep me satisfied. I never looked back, and all foods were on the plate, so to speak.
I really don't remember the "awakening" to the food opportunities since I was only about 5 months old. It has been a great journey, so far!

Now, 74 years later, I'm not sure I have ever been hungry—but I enjoy eating to keep from getting hungry. I am fine with Beans and Taters, BBQ and hushpuppies, Chicken Soup and

Crackers, Steak and Salads, homemade Bread is a particular weakness of mine. You get the picture.

With my addiction it has been a great benefit to me to have learned how to prepare and cook (or bake) almost anything I want. I make a mean Blackberry Cobbler and have had many great reviews on my Black Walnut cake. No one has ever turned down one of my home-grown, grass-fed, Rib Eye steaks, grilled to perfection, either.

My first memory of helping cook was building a fire under our large wash pot, drawing water from the well, heating it so Mom could wash clothes with her wringer washing machine. I was probably about 7 years old, and although it was not really cooking, you have to learn to boil water first, right!

When I was around 14, Dad would take me to work with him in the summertime. My job was to set up and build a fire under the legged frying pan and cook fish for his customers. He was the bartender at the county line beer joint. Evidently Beer and Fish just naturally go together. I never tried the combination since I had already quit drinking, but I did like the fish.

I dearly remember each year when our sweet corn would ripen to the roast-n-ear stage. We would shuck a big batch and boil it up. Boy was it good with home churned butter and salt. We would make a meal out of that, and, buddy, it was hard to beat!

The biggest disappointment I ever experienced with food was home-made Ice Cream. It was the spring of 1965, probably late March or early April. It had been a beautiful spring with lots of rain, so the pastures were greening up nicely. Then it turned very warm. Tim, one of our neighbors had stopped by one Saturday, and while talking about the unusually warm weather the subject of Ice Cream came up. We got excited about the prospects, but the problem was that our Cow had died the past year, and we had no milk. Tim's family had a small dairy herd, and he offered to go home, skim the cream from one of the large metal milk cans and contribute that to our ingredients for the treat. While he was gone, we cleaned up the dasher and tub, busted up some of the ice that we kept in the freezer, measured the sugar and vanilla flavoring, got the salt ready to put on the ice and were ready to make Ice Cream. We were getting more excited by the minute. With all ingredients combined, we started cranking the handle. It usually takes a long, long hour to get the proper freeze, so we took turns slowly turning the handle over and over.

The anticipation grew with each turn of the handle. After what seemed like eternity it was ready. We dipped out bowlfuls and passed them around. It seems like everyone took a bite at the same time.

IT WAS AWFUL!

As any farm boy knows, the first green thing to come up in the spring is Wild Onions, and they had comprised a large portion of the cow's diet. I have often stated that the difference between a cook and a chef is the amount of onions he uses. I learned the hard way a long time ago that statement does not apply to Ice Cream. •

Taste the Disappointment

Copyright 2025, Joe Brown

Joe Brown is a retired building contractor. He lives on a small family farm in the Bethania area of Winston Salem NC. He now has time to do all those projects that a busy work schedule didn't allow.
He enjoys his grandchildren and great grandchildren and as time allows likes to reflect on his life and write stories about his adventures. Several of those stories have been shared through the Personal Publishing Project. His prayer is that his family can appreciate the history he has lived.

Tenderfoot
by Bob Amason

I made a stupid move one day in April 1972. I walked into my college buddy Ken Osborne's room at Georgia Tech and said, "Let's go backpacking."

Never being one to turn down such an insane idea, Oz immediately replied, "Ok! How about Saturday? We'll go to Mount LeConte in the Smoky Mountains."

So started our tenderfoot backpacking trip.

I inaccurately concluded that Oz knew all things backpacking. After all, he had a ratty canvas backpack with a nice metal frame. The well-used pack indicated deep experience. I was to learn otherwise…in detail.

Thirty-five hard-earned dollars at Sears got me a bright yellow backpack emblazoned with Sir Edmund Hillary's heroic visage. It was either him or baseball great Ted Williams. I went with Sir Edmund.

The pack had a metal frame and a hip belt. If ol' Sir Edmund could climb Mount Everest with this pack, I could make it up the 6,593-foot Mount LeConte. I was cookin' with gas! (Well, not really, but more on that in a moment).

I bought a pair of chukka boots at K-Mart for $5. Perfect for a long hike up a mountain, right?

We threw cans of food in our backpacks and got ready to slog up that hill! We each had one of those 1960s sleeping bags made of heavy cotton. You know, the kind that sweats you in the summer and freezes you in the winter? Yep, that kind. We would show our woodcraft by building a cooking fire for the Dinty Moore Beef Stew and other delicacies we carried. I had a can of Vienna sausage in there somewhere.

The Mount LeConte parking lot was full, so we parked illegally on the road, refusing to let mere park regulations deter our intrepid journey to glory. We marched the half mile to the hilariously named Boulevard Trail, the gateway to the sparkling vistas awaiting us atop scenic Mount LeConte.

Undeterred by the 8.1-mile distance, which appeared straight up, we tromped along in our chukka boots. Yes, Oz had chukka boots, too. He inspired my footwear selection.

Later, we traversed a couple of places on the trail where the hiker must hold onto a cable to keep from plunging over a sheer drop just inches away. Undaunted, we scoffed at the potential to dive into oblivion down a Tennessee mountainside. Likewise, in our naïveté, we gave an enthusiastic, if foolish, nod to wearing slick, gum-soled chukka boots and a pack filled with heavy canned goods.

Exhausted and foot-sore, we reached the peak and were disappointed to discover it was 100 percent shrouded in clouds.

All that work and poor planning to reach the top only to be thwarted by Mother Nature. *Bitch*.

We dumped our stuff in a shelter with a chain-link fence across the front. A guy lounging on a lightweight goose-down sleeping bag and snacking on granola explained that the fence was there to keep bears out. He also said that Mount LeConte was almost always shrouded in clouds. So much for our planned vistas.

Tenderfoot was 100% accurate - those chukka boots were miserable for anything other than a cruise around Atlanta's Lennox Square Mall. Worse, the sleeping bags were clammy, having wicked up about 10 pounds of the moisture swirling around the summit. We built a fire from wet, green sticks and filled the shelter with acrid smoke, earning the side-eye from fellow campers. An experienced camper said, "God's sake, buy a Primus gas stove." We nodded sagely as though we knew what that was.

I ate cold, greasy Dinty Moore and rummaged in my Sir Edmund Hillary pack to find sufficient funds to buy a Coke and a Hershey Bar at the LeConte Lodge, a venerable, rustic place. That was the best meal of my weekend. Not the stew, the candy bar. Sadly, the lodge had no vacancies.

On the way down the hill, we rounded a curve to find a mama bear and her cubs. We turned and hot-footed it back up the hill a hundred yards and began surveying which trees we might climb. A 12-year-old kid rounded the curve in the trail. He was coming from Bear Country! Naturally, we asked if he saw the bear. The kid snorted, and said, "Yeah, right," and kept walking. I distinctly heard him call us a word that ended in "holes," but I'm unsure. Kids these days…

I sheepishly donned my Sir Edmund Hillary backpack with custom mesh back support and specially padded hip belt. We marched resolutely toward where Mama Bear was last seen. Thank God, she was gone.

We approached the highway, where a small rushing creek beckoned. I dropped Sir Edmund, dumped the chukkas, and stuck my boiling feet in the fresh, freezing mountain water. My poor feet smiled, and I smiled, too.

We had conquered the daunting Mount LeConte, tender feet and all. •

Copyright 2025, Bob Amason

Award-winning author Bob Amason is a retired US Air Force Lieutenant Colonel who was a college professor for 25 years. A Florida Writer's Association member, Bob writes historical and modern suspense novels under his pen name, Frank A. Mason. His *Journeyman Chronicles* series on the American Revolutionary War won the 2023 Florida Writer's Association's prestigious Gold Royal Palm Literary Award. Bob's writing has been published in six anthologies, academic journals, and books. Dr. Bob Amason lives in Florida with his overachieving wife, a research professor and author of a series of children's books.

We Got Five Done
by Howard Pearre

I had taken a do-it-yourself automotive repair course at the community college. So, when a friend from work said he was having problems with his car—sputtering, dying while idling at a stoplight, cutting out when he was trying to blend into interstate traffic—I knew just what to do.

"Pick up a set of spark plugs at Advance and come on over tonight after work," I told Ronnie. "I know what to do."

The course's curriculum had been simple: bring your car in, open the hood and tinker away, or pop the hubcaps, wrestle the wheel off, and tinker away. The instructor wore grease-stained coveralls and wandered around giving individual instruction on how to change the oil, do a brake job, clean a dirty carburetor, or change spark plugs. They even had a hydraulic lift, so you didn't have to crawl under your car to change the oil.

I put new brake shoes on my car, rotated the tires, changed the spark plugs, and, using the community college's professional-grade timing light, gave it a tune up. My '68 Rambler hummed.

I bought an $11 timing light from Advance Auto Parts—it cost only $11 for a reason—and a spark plug gap gauge so I could take care of business on my own.

Ronnie showed up with a new set of Champions and pulled into my carport. He said he'd bought the car used about a year ago and didn't know if the spark plugs ever had been changed.

The first task was to extract the old ones. I unhooked the spark plug wire caps and inserted the first one into a socket attached to a 9-inch extension rod on my ratchet wrench. I carefully pulled the wrench handle toward me. The plug responded, and I showed it to Ronnie.

"This wasn't helping," I said. The plug's two gap points were covered with black gunk.

When the next plug did not respond, I gave it a gentle bump and pulled the wrench handle a little harder. Nothing.

"Maybe some Liquid Wrench will do the trick," I said ducking my head to avoid a nasty encounter with the open hood.

I retrieved the can of penetrating oil from my toolbox, gave the base of the stuck plug a generous dose, and let it seep in for a few minutes. After the treatment, the plug loosened.

"Works like a charm," I told Ronnie.

I squirted the remaining plugs with the magic formula, waited, and extracted numbers four, five, and six with ease.

"That third one, it's just darn stubborn," I said, squirting more penetrating oil into the crevice at the base of the plug.

We waited and tried the socket wrench again. It was more than stubborn. It was stuck.

"*Whatchagonnado?*" Ronnie asked.

"Got just the ticket. Wait here."

I remembered seeing a galvanized pipe, about four feet long, in the crawl space of my house that must have been left over from a plumbing job.

When I returned, Ronnie was busy gapping the new plugs.

"Here we go. With this as an extension to the wrench handle, that baby will pop right out."

I placed the socket back onto the stuck plug and inserted the wrench handle into the pipe.

"Okay, Mr. Spark Plug. Out you come."

Slowly, I applied pressure to the pipe. The plug did not budge. I applied a little more pressure. Nothing. I gave it another dose of penetrating oil, waited, and pulled a little harder.

There was a soft crunch sound, and the pipe moved toward me. The sound and the easy flexibility of the pipe in my hand gave me a sick feeling.

I lifted the pipe and wrench away. Part of the spark plug was in the socket. The rest of it was still in the engine block.

"Ronnie, I think I just messed up," I said, unnecessarily, as Ronnie uttered a short gasp. It took us 30 minutes more to insert five of the new plugs in the engine block, but I did not know what to do to get the bottom half of the last one out. Also, no need now for the timing-light tune up procedure.

I offered to give Ronnie the $60 he would need to pay a real mechanic to fix my mistake, but Ronnie said no. He said I'd done my best.

"Well, at least we got five done," he said

Ronnie chugged home that night on the car's five working cylinders and had to come in late the next day after taking his car in for the repair. He didn't say anything more about his car, but when we went out to lunch, I bought him a Big Mac and large fries. •

Copyright 2025, Howard Pearre

Howard Pearre lives in Winston-Salem, North Carolina. He attended UNC Charlotte and Appalachian State University and retired after a career as a counselor and manager with NC Vocational Rehabilitation and the US Department of Veterans Affairs. He served in the Army as a paratrooper and is a 5k runner. His essays and fiction have appeared in *Flying South*, the *Dead Mule School of Southern Literature*, *Proud To Be*, and other publications.

Close Call
by Erika Hoffman

While we were enjoying breakfast at a hotel in California, a pleasant lady promised us a three-night stay at a reduced price at a popular beach if we'd listen to a 90-minute spiel.

"I'd rather not," I told my husband.

"We won't buy in," he said.

"Let's not...," I repeated.

"We'll just listen."

Eighteen months later, after checking into the efficiency suite the night before, we had to be at the presentation at 8:15 a.m. We summoned our car. (A valet was required; a nightly fee was added.) It took thirty minutes for the car to be brought round.

We had a short drive to the sales venue. Everyone exuded hospitality. The sales rep, Ms. B from AZ, introduced herself. We made a connection. My cousins live in Arizona. Secondly, she was a grandma, like me. She had three sons, like me. She escorted us into a dark room for a power point presentation, led by a Dolly Parton doppelganger, so charming she could sell a bald man a comb! She told a heart-wrenching story of having been deathly sick, of fostering a child later put up for adoption, how she hadn't seen the girl for a decade, and one day the girl found her again. They made up for lost time by taking spectacular trips to scenic places. Their smiling faces lit up the screen. We left the room with a lift in our step buoyed up by this heartwarming and happily-ever-after ending. *Thank goodness for timeshare points! Amen!* The message landed.

Ms. B. led us through a series of prairie dog cubicles, passing by smiling, quick-talking reps and captive couples. The reps—animated. The couples enraptured. Several times, my husband complimented Ms. B on what a great salesperson she was. Ms. B shared anecdotal tales about her grandchildren. Those stories resonated. She told us about clients she'd met who were difficult and… "totally unlike us."

I reiterated we weren't going to buy a timeshare. I didn't want to waste her time. My husband listened to the advantages this timeshare would provide us—fabulous resorts at a fraction of the price. The points we'd buy would never go down.

"Your dream destination?" she asked.

"Australia," I replied.

Dutifully, she jotted it down. "Tell me what you like best about our program."

"We can resell it to you if it doesn't work out; we can recoup some of our money."

"Or you sell it to a neighbor," chimed in her business partner Larry, who joined us.

"I'm worried about leaving a timeshare to our kids. They'd be obligated to pay housekeeping fees and assessments," I said.

"This isn't a timeshare. Our program's based on points."

"Could we put it in an LLC?" inserted my husband.

"Why not?" said Larry.

"We'll get you some new credit cards," one chimed in. "You could charge the cost of it on them."

I had a terrible cold. I left four times to blow my nose. Before I'd leave, I'd say ominously, "I hope this is only a cold." Every time I returned, we were offered more points to sweeten the deal ... or some "swag."

Hours later, Ms. B announced, "I'll leave you alone so you can decide."

"You decide," I said to my spouse. "I don't want a timeshare. Yet, if you can get your money back, then it sounds safer than most."

"That's what she said."

Ms. B returned, carrying a stack of papers for us to sign. We had one more step— to visit the compliance officer.

"She'll have a few questions," Ms. B said dismissively.

We thanked her; she disappeared.

We sat across from "Darlene" and a hill of papers. We initialed obediently, wherever Darlene pointed. Then, she turned to where Ms. B had written the reasons for our buying a timeshare: 1.) vacations. 2.) something to leave our children. 3.) other options.

"Other options?" I asked. "The third reason was that we can sell it back to the timeshare owners if it doesn't work out."

Darlene tilted her head sideways, peering at me wryly. "You don't have any guarantee of getting any money back."

"*What?*"

Close Call

"We have first right of refusal before you can sell it to anyone else, but we won't look to buy it."

"That's not what we were told," my husband said.

"Who told you otherwise?" asked Darlene.

"They both did," we said.

Ms. B lurked. Darlene called her in. Ms. B said she'd have to find Larry. Larry returned and denied he'd said that. We were flabbergasted. After he left, Darlene said she'd rip up the papers.

"I feel bad for Ms. B," I said.

"Don't," said Darlene.

Ms. B re-appeared. Darlene stated we weren't buying the timeshare.

Ms. B's lips turned down. Her eyes squinted. Her whole demeanor changed. She cast a menacing glance toward the compliance agent. She didn't look at us. She left without saying good-bye to us, her newfound BFFs.

I expected Ms. B might snap her fingers and announce dramatically, *Curses! Foiled again!* •

Copyright 2025, Erika Hoffman

Erika Hoffman is a happy and longtime resident of beautiful North Carolina. She's a member of three writing clans: North Carolina Writers Network; The Triangle Area Freelancers; and Carteret Writers. During the past 14 years while pursuing "her scrivener dream," she has succeeded in getting published 481 times. Yet, Erika deems her best achievement— besides being married forever—is having raised four functioning citizens. Without a doubt, her proudest moniker is "Ama" to six grandsons and four granddaughters.

Proper Punishment for an Old Offender
by Paula Teem Levi

Stanley Oyler awoke on March 13, 1930, feeling that 13 was a lucky number for him. He was getting married to Virginia Brown, his longtime girlfriend, in Huntington, West Virginia.

Because a small group of family and friends had gathered to celebrate the marriage, Stanley decided after the ceremony to drive his mother's 1925 Packard automobile to Charleston to purchase some liquor. On the way back to the party, he was stopped by a revenue agent and arrested on prohibition charges.

Following his conviction eight months later, Judge George W. McClintic of the United States District Court, Charleston, West Virginia recommended the following, according to *The Charleston Gazette:*

> Thirty-nine lashes laid on the bare back by a big deputy sheriff would be, in the opinion of the judge, the proper punishment for Stanley Oyler, Charleston, who is an old offender in the court.
>
> Oyler couldn't remember yesterday how many times he had been sentenced in federal court, and the judge said that he was "tired of sending" Oyler away. Oyler's plea

of guilty to possessing untaxed liquor was taken under advisement until November 29.

Oyler reported that he got out of prison last January, got married in March, got some liquor for a wedding celebration, and got caught.

On November 29, 1930, Stanley Oyler was sentenced to three years in the Atlanta Federal Penitentiary and was fined $200. He received one of the longest prison terms and one of the highest monetary fines because he was a repeat offender.

A front-page story in *The Charleston Gazette* that December told the story of Stanley and others being sent off to prison:

> **Eighty Depart, Atlanta Bound**
> Federal Prisoners March Through Streets as Curious Stare
>
> Bound for Atlanta Federal Penitentiary, 80 prisoners were removed from Charleston yesterday morning aboard four special coaches attached to a Chesapeake and Ohio passenger train.
>
> Yesterday's Atlanta bound contingent of 80 was arranged in a column of shackled couples in the alley at the rear of the city jail by several deputies and a staff of special guards. All but four of the contingent of 80 were sentenced on prohibition charges.
>
> Under the cynical, curious, or sorrowing eyes of strangers and relatives, the 80 men were marched briskly through Court and Kanawha Streets to the South Side Bridge and thence to the special coaches attached to the passenger train on the sidetrack below the passenger station. At least 100 friends, relatives and

idlers followed the prisoners to the station. At one point, the parade passed by a clicking motion picture.

Some of the 80 had the furtive, disheveled jail-bird air about them, but most of them had done their best to present a decent appearance during their brief quarter of an hour in the public eye. Some muttered curses at the bold stares of the idlers who followed the parade. Others had a smile and a wave of their free hand for their friends and kin.

The C. and O. train dropped the coaches at Lexington, where an L. and N. engine picked them up, and run them inside the prison walls at Atlanta about noon today.

Stanley's letters to his mother and wife spoke of life in the Atlanta Federal Penitentiary as "being dreary." He wrote, "The inmates here are an army of forgotten men who have been traumatized by the violence, harsh conditions and isolation."

Prohibition ended with the ratification at the federal level of the Twenty-First Amendment on December 5, 1933. Five days later, Stanley was paroled from the Atlanta Federal Penitentiary after serving out his sentence.

Readjusting to life after incarceration was challenging. Stanley found it hard to forget the violence and conditions he had endured in prison. Shortly after he left prison, his wife divorced him.

Trying to find employment with a criminal record and to gain financial stability was frustrating for Stanley. He accepted the rejections and focused on making a successful transition from his rogue, racketeering life.

He avoided his old neighborhood and patterns that had landed him in prison so many times. He began volunteering in a community program sponsored by a church that mentored at-risk youth. He wanted to help curb youths from making bad choices that would lead them down the same destructive paths that he had followed.

In late January, Stanley got a job as a laborer at his old place of employment. With stable employment, he could then focus on beginning his new life.

In early March only a month or so later, Stanley was admitted to a Charleston hospital. He died near the end of March from complications of Addison's Disease. His sister, Goldie, said, "Stanley was given a chance at redemption, though fleeting. He had proven himself to be a productive member of society."

Stanley had great expectations for turning his life around, but he ran out of time. •

Copyright 2025, Paula Teem Levi

Paula Teem Levi is a retired Registered Nurse living in Clover, South Carolina. She is a member of several genealogical societies. Her stories have appeared in seven previous anthologies of the Personal Story Publishing Project. "Who's That Lady," which appeared in *Curious Stuff*, recently received an Award of Excellence from the North Carolina Society of Historians. Her goal is to preserve as many family stories as possible for future generations so that they will not be at risk of being forgotten or lost forever.

A Debt of Gratitude
by Randell Jones

We all die with some accounts in arrears. For certain, we leave behind debts of gratitude we never get to repay. By the time we mature enough to know this, those we want to thank—need to thank, ought to thank—have likely passed on. That's just the way life works.

We are left with paying it forward, which probably makes for a better world, but is not as personally satisfying as getting to close the loop with the people who helped us. So, it's special when we can.

The theme for this collection of personal stories is "Foiled—great expectations gone awry by surprise, short-sightedness, and trickery." After we collected the stories and I knew what trials and tribulations, what successes by overcoming challenging odds, what fears, what tears, what laughs, what love writers had decided to share with the world, then somehow, I would have to create a book cover that wrapped its artistic arms around everyone and all stories—a tall order, for sure.

The "foiled" image I sought might suggest a blocking of forward motion, a curtailment of momentum, an interruption of inertia. A simple stop sign would suffice for that. But the stories were about continuing on, working around the obstacles, getting things done despite being thwarted. The protagonists kept moving. What about their stories? What was that image?

Scrolling, scrolling, scrolling through images online, and then there it was—a simple humanoid figure fashioned from aluminum foil. (Foil, get it?). I clicked on the image and was transported Alice-in-Wonderland-like, tumbling down a rabbit hole of artwork and creations all made of aluminum foil. Such a hole in cyberspace has no bottom, of course, so I grabbed onto one protruding root—to overtax the Alice-falling metaphor—and pulled myself over to the side, to one site—*Mrs. Knight's Smartest Artists*. Clever name. Remarkable teacher.

Here was a trove of art ideas for classroom teachers in elementary schools, and I had happened upon one of hundreds, her project for making figures from aluminum foil. The photographs were prolific of successful creations. One class was making human figures holding popsicle-stick swords. But these were not crafted from students' imaginations. Standing on top of a desk in the middle of the 4th grade classroom was a classmate posing with a plastic sword. These students were doing art from live models. *What a hoot!* What a confidence booster for the artists. What an inspiration for other teachers. Good on you, Mrs. Knight.

I kept scrolling through the pictures until I found a few aluminum foil forms of interest, all from her 2014 portfolio. She had been doing this for years, I saw. And other art teachers from schools around the country were thanking her and telling about their successful uses of her ideas.

I selected a picture of a human figure standing on one leg. It had no discernable face, so I could not tell if it was looking down like a performing figure skater gliding gracefully with arms outstretched for balance or was it looking up, frozen amidst a prat fall, a slipping-on-the-banana-peel moment, with arms flailing out to the side, grasping for something to catch onto. For me, it captured perfectly "great expectations gone awry." Here we are in our lives performing with hopes and dreams when something unexpected happens, something we cannot control. We flail about for balance, we fall, we get up (we hope) but our plans in that moment are changed. We learn, we adjust, we try again.

I decided to ask Mrs. Knight if I could use the picture. I found an email address at the website. I noticed the portfolios continued until 2022 and then stopped. I checked her blog and found that she had retired in March of that year. *Well, darn, too late.* I saw pictures of her retirement cake with teachers and staff gathered around, saying goodbye. I also read her note to students saying that she was retiring because of a serious health problem.

I googled Mrs. Knight by full name. Her obituary slapped me hard. She died in November 2022. She was 55.

I had wanted to ask her for the possible use of the image and to thank her. I expected to, just as she expected to continue sparking the light of creativity in the minds of young students for another dozen years, as any of us would, certain in the belief that we will surely get more time—more time because we are busy, more time because we are doing good things, more time because we want it. *Shouldn't we?*

A Debt of Gratitude

That's just not the way life works. We know that even as we keep performing, learning from each fall.

So, instead:
Congratulations on your teaching career, Mrs. Knight. You helped thousands of students in your 26-year career and inspired people in ways you would never know. You helped me, and I just wanted to say *thank you*. I hope you like the book cover. It is the perfect image. And every reader will think of you when they see it.

Blessings on those who knew you, loved you, miss you still. Blessings on those who are grateful for having been inspired by you, but maybe did not get around to telling you so. Perhaps they will pay it forward.

Godspeed. •

Copyright 2025, Randell Jones

Randell Jones is an award-winning writer about the pioneer and Revolutionary War eras and North Carolina history. During 25 years, he has written 150+ history-based guest columns for the *Winston-Salem Journal*. His newest release is the expanded 2nd edition of the 2005 biography and travel guide, *In the Footsteps of Daniel Boone* (2024) and the related video, *Boone's America: Boone Trace, 1775*. In 2017, he created the Personal Story Publishing Project and in 2019, the companion podcast, "6-minute Stories" to encourage other writers. He lives in Winston-Salem, North Carolina. Visit *RandellJones.com* and *BecomingAmerica250.com*.

www.ingramcontent.com/pod-product-compliance
Lightning Source LLC
Chambersburg PA
CBHW020232170426
43201CB00007B/403